OUR MEZZOGIORNO
Selected Writings by Luca and Friends

NICOLETTA STAME, EDITOR
A Colorni-Hirschman International Institute

Translated by Michael Gilmartin

BORDIGHERA PRESS
NEW YORK

Il nostro mezzogiorno
Volume 3

This book series is dedicated to the presentation of new perspectives on how we might re-consider Southern Italy.

COVER ART: Pythagoras and Archimedes, detail from Raphael's *The School of Athens* in the Apostolic Palace, Vatican City, 1509–1511

ISBN 978-1-59954-207-2
Library of Congress Control Number: 2025937726

BORDIGHERA PRESS
NEW YORK

TABLE OF CONTENTS

"Our Mezzogiorno"

INTRODUCTION

> [Meldolesi's essay on labor mobility] is "a document surprising for its novelty, to be read like travelogues in unknown lands used to be (...) Out of it emerges unexpectedly a 'path of hope' toward the creation of a society based on a market economy even in the Mezzogiorno. An intuition (...) supported by 'discoveries' that seem to echo those of modern historiographical archaeology, which by analyzing layers of soil and shards is capable of finding and studying the historical relics of earlier complex civilizations. In our case, researchers have devoted themselves to a veritable 'hunt for businesses down the block.' " — Mario Pirani

1. MEZZOGIORNO AND VERTICALISM

This collection presents the group's mission statement in its general conception and shows how it has played out in terms of analysis and policy initiative. "Possibilist," democratic, and anti-verticalist in inspiration, it is centered on the Mezzogiorno, the case under study. But the Mezzogiorno also represents the archetype of a middle-of-the-scale situation — it is not underdeveloped, but nor is it the democratic market-economy society that it would like to become. ("A southern society that has its own productive life based mostly on small business, but which is turned in upon itself, clinging to types of behavior that only partly correspond to the democratic market economy system we intend to build" [ch. 7]).

Its ambition is to achieve a mastery of the situation and a progressive reduction of hierarchical structures "through processes that *enhance what is beautiful and good* — that is, innovation, prosperity, democracy, social justice, gender equality, science, art, etc. — which can play a role as a 'magnet,' and, at the same time, as a triggering, liberating factor of the great, extraordinary human energies that relations of domination unfortunately keep in check." But to be a magnet for this "potential cause of the dependent world," we need to act intelligently with respect to the spontaneous tendency to feel equal to those above us (verticalist analysis, horizontalist desire) without caring who follows us — not imitating the top but valuing the bottom. "Instead of elevating ourselves by pressing down on those below us, we need to turn around and give them a hand, so that we can progress together" (ch. 1).

The underlying idea is to look at Southern society through a lens of complexity — seeing the totality of positive and negative aspects, economic and psychological, along with a practical and democratic economic policy that takes into account both poles of these dichotomies, is capable of combating the negative aspects (the scourges) and valuing the positive ones (industriousness, the traditional values of work, thrift, and saving (ch. 3), and which takes into account the psychological fallout from economic measures (which may increase or decrease welfarist tendencies). The aim is to "strengthen pro-development behavior (whether of peasant, artisan or "cultured" origin) and combat negative behavior (the three scourges), either directly or through the indirect effect of economic forces" (ch. 7), and "to intervene punctually in an anti-pathological key by intelligently promoting positive processes, whatever social and political form they take. It is delicate and complex work that requires a good deal of 'possibilist' training" (ch. 4).

This central inspirational core is then articulated in many different branches, each time gaining in the breadth of the reality observed, and in the depth of the reasoning.[1]

In the previous volume we have seen how this experiment came about in a university context that was particularly open to the outside world (*An Education*); in the next one we will look at its main analytical and methodological contributions to studies of the Southern setting and local development (*A Practical and Democratic Social Science*). While these books provide the reference material for understanding how such an approach matured, this volume deals more specifically with how the change in the image of the Mezzogiorno that is thus postulated (surprise, analytical possibilism) leads to a necessary reorientation of development policy (a different Meridionalism, propositional possibilism).

2.   THE CHANGING IMAGE OF THE MEZZOGIORNO

How is the image of the Mezzogiorno changing? We find out from "operation truth" (ch. 1). It is no longer entirely negative (a "ball and chain" by comparison with the "developed and industrial" North; populated by lazy people and *Camorristi*), but rather a complex of rapidly developing productive centers conditioned by pathological behavior patterns (ch. 4). Rather than a wasteland of unemployment requiring job-creation, it is a land teeming with small and medium-sized industrial activities asking for support. And it is energized by a will to emerge, expressed by young people who have come to embrace the possibility of changing the "balance of behavior" (between rising entrepreneurship and the rationale of the permanent job), and have had a glimpse of new possibilities.

---

[1] This is a reference to the Hirschmanian method assimilated by Luca — focus on one problem, one aspect, and drill down into that. Then broaden the gaze to other neighboring areas, to other disciplines.

The construction of this image comes with a desire to dig deep, to look at things as they are—fact finding, yes, but with great empathy as well. We need to be able to make distinctions within the mix of legal and illegal behavior, operating in full legality and developing flexible tactics. We need to understand the meaning of "asymmetry in favor of the private sphere," and how it relates to the "proclivity for light industrialization" that resulted in the development of the production of Made-in-Italy merchandise (for the person and the home). This is where semi-submerged businesses and mixed labor relations are created, arrangements that need to be developed for their potential, not repressed for their shortcomings. This is the image of a Mezzogiorno composed of "a myriad of small businesses alongside medium and larger ones," and of Southerners who "are in the great majority a population of ants who get up early in the morning to go to work." (ch. 5). The exploration of this Mezzogiorno, pursued with the help of students, is driven by a "passion for possible change," which includes overcoming pessimism and implosive tendencies, keeping at bay the anthropomorphic tendency to superimpose individual and collective desires on the understanding of reality, and initiating positive ventures and actions (as was the case with students who wrote 'super-theses,' or those who took up entrepreneurship).

3. A DIFFERENT MERIDIONALISM

The observations on semi-submerged and diffuse entrepreneurship areas, in addition to presenting a situation that eludes traditional categorization, invites us to envision policies that are alternative to both the old Meridionalism of large scale public spending (the policy of subsidies—bridging the North-South gap through public investment, which fosters corruption, clientelism and corporatism) and the new Meridionalism focused on labor policy but failing to take into account the existence of the dual labor market (ch. 9). Both cases, albeit for different reasons, prefigure welfarism.

Our Mezzogiorno's practical and democratic economic policy, in contrast, has to be based on a decision once and for all to deal courageously (and honestly)[2] with the issues raised, and on an *administration* capable of responsibly facilitating, overseeing, evaluating and adjusting the developments that would result. It is this that lies behind all the group's work, beginning with "A Framework for the South," (ch. 7) a text from 1992 offering a development strategy that takes into account the economic and behavioral effects-both for the beneficiaries and for the administration of the intervention tools available. This stakes out the junctures (automatic/indirect; empowering/involving; responsible/directed) that "allow the dangers of clientelist brokering to be minimized".

Subsequently, and based on experience, this analysis was supplemented by highly detailed proposals regarding the tools to be used, to wit — "a whole set of measures relating to a wide range of problems," "used serially or jointly" in different economic and social sectors.[3] It is a real "project for emergence"[4] (), formulated following a method in which possibilism figures in the proposal — which "put[s] forward the argument as concretely as possible, almost as if to create the illusion

---

[2] "The long-term concealment of the reality of the Southern submerged economy out of misunderstood pride or craftiness has seriously harmed the interest of the South, the country and European edifice itself" (ch. 7).

[3] The "First Report of the National Committee," (ch. 9) for example, lists many different measures for specific sectors such as domestic work, construction, tourism, old-age pensioners, etc.

[4] The "Basic Outline for an Emergence Project" (ch. 8) is an article summarizing many of the proposals that matured during that period; the "First Report of the National Committee " (ch. 9), which takes up and articulates many of those proposals, is an official document that states that it can "be taken as a starting point for certain legislative initiatives."

that it could be put into practice tomorrow morning" (ch. 8). The difficulties are known, but we embrace the desire for change and indicate feasible ways forward.

Proposals are categorized as local and direct, or centralized and indirect.

Local and direct measures are the focus of general attention—e.g., territorial agreements or European Structural Funds—but they are also those in which a diversion of public funds to other purposes is easier. It is here that we often witness the sort of distorted situation in which planning proceeds as if the submerged economy did not exist (and newly financed businesses did not reflect the double economy). As if, that is, the issue was simply a lack of enterprise (and not of consolidating the most prominent developments in semi-submerged entrepreneurship that already exist). It is here that "a practical planning effort [is needed,] based on actual knowledge of the situation on the ground"[5] along with administrative work to set up "simple implementation procedures [...] that establish priorities and alternative advantages (...) [and] put in place both a monitoring mechanism linked to operational accounting and a follow-up of *ex post* evaluation as a basis for the recurrent reorganization of the different policy interventions" (ch. 8). These are issues that require broad mobilization—the creation of new instruments such as local service centers (in cooperation with craft and business associations and aimed at upgrading existing entrepreneurship), organize administrators along the lines of a task force, and involve the beneficiaries.

Central and indirect policy actions cover the workings of the market, reductions in the tax burden, safety regulations, social security, and justice. All these are areas in which the

---

[5] In this regard, the "First Report" (ch. 9) speaks of "*territorial pacts aimed at emergence,* providing for the establishment on the ground of special *development centers*" (p. 175).

state can adopt ad hoc measures for the Mezzogiorno, but differentiated by territorial, sectoral and labor conditions, and always with negotiated deadlines and regular checks on the degree of regularization achieved.

More generally, placing the semi-submerged economy at the center of the new image of the Mezzogiorno means that the policy of regularization can become a catalyst for the possibility of change throughout the country, showing how a "friendly state that can't be cheated" might work. A state, in other words, "that dispenses trust, cooperation, escape routes, etc., but only until there is proof to the contrary, and in order to head this off, continually updates a database of each citizen's benefits and fiscal behavior." (ch. 9). In the case of the semi-submerged economy, this would involve the combined use of sanction and promotion, aiming at regularization as the outcome and constantly evaluating the progress achieved, so as to support developmental practices and counteract welfarist relapses. It would mean taking responsibility for the interests of the beneficiaries, the productivity of the supported business, and the fairness of the conditions under which the work is provided, etc. In other words, devising ad hoc measures for each specific situation and feeling responsible for seeing that they are not overturned.

4. EVERYONE CAN CONTRIBUTE TO THE CHANGE

The picture sketched out in this way calls upon many different actors, all of whom can contribute to change by doing their part.

Southerners must overcome their sense of inadequacy regarding the North, but also their sense of superiority over other Souths, and the idea that their own area is exceptional with respect to other Southern contexts. This is why they would do well to compare themselves with other environments, as "The Mezzogiorno and East Germany" (ch. 3) suggests.

Development scholars need to break free from patterns developed elsewhere on which they base their ideas of conditions and obstacles and take a closer look at how local agents use (or fail to use) the resources available to them (ch. 5). They will find an unexpected vitality with distinctive characteristics, and they will need to equip themselves to engage with it.

Statisticians need to change not only their survey criteria (questions, interviewers), but also their assumptions and their categories — e.g., recognizing that behind someone who claims to be "unemployed" or outside the labor force is a person who, while working a semi-submerged job, aspires to a regular, permanent position (ch. 6).

But even those who have a fixed job (permanent contract, government job) should not view it as an annuity, but should feel that they are part of an effort towards improvement and increased productivity and toward providing service that is attentive to the needs of the recipients.

Decision makers need to develop policies that take into account the facts of specific situations, lest a general rule should lend itself to a specific distorted interpretation — labor legislation must take into account the dual labor market,[6] and business legislation the dual accounting. But subsequently the success of such policies will also depend on what the administrators do. Knowing the world in which the policies will be applied, they should feel committed to understanding the needs of businesses, devising practices — even gradual — that encourage regularization and discourage any spontaneous tendency to further submerge.

---

[6] For example, realignment contracts, which have been applied differently in Campania and Puglia, and only in particular sectors.

THE INTUITION

1. VERTICALISM AND MAGNETS[*]

1 - [...]The suspicion is legitimate that the most genuine, long-term interest of the Mezzogiorno and of Italy as a whole — and, for that matter, of the vast world of small and medium-sized countries and of the many "dependent" peoples living in the different regions of the world — does not actually lie in an economic (political, military, cultural, etc.) race that will ultimately lead to some eventual changing of the guard at the top of the system — that is, to a pure and simple reconfiguration and readjustment of the economic-political pyramidal structure of the planet.[1] On the contrary, it would appear that what is fundamentally needed is an effort to master and progressively reduce such hierarchical arrangements through processes that *enhance what is beautiful and good* — in other words, innovation, prosperity, democracy, social justice, gender equality, science, art, etc. — which can play a role as a 'magnet,' and, at the same time, as a triggering, liberating factor of the great, extraordinary human energies that relations of domination unfortunately keep in check.[2]

It would then be a matter of taking on board, but also vigorously correcting, the spontaneous tendencies that already exist, but also of "starting somewhere" — to show *urbi et orbi*, in ways and forms to be identified (and put into practice as we go

---

[*] From Luca Meldolesi (2021a), "Introduction", *Mezzogiorno. Mezzomondo*, p. 14-29.
[1] In which, from the UN on down, the formal equality of peoples and countries barely manages to coexist with the substantial, often abysmal, inequalities that divide them.
[2] If not actually frustrating and dissipating them, these energies — more or less consciously. Undoubtedly, it would be a fitting task for a country such as ours that is without peer, but which over time is being relatively (but inevitably) scaled down, partly due to the indirect effect of the comparative awakening of many countries more populous than ours.

along), that... the game really is worth the effort, as was shown by our first (and decisive) attempt to move in that direction. It was an unexpected "test," enabled by a constellation of circumstances,[3] which had behind it an important international collaboration and an intense effort of study, training and field research by an amazing and outstanding group of young undergraduates and graduate students.[4]

It has been followed by other experiences of similar inspiration[5] that have kept alive, however discontinuously, the vast Italian (and Italic[6]) circle, predominantly southern, scattered across the five continents, in an age — as ours is — of increasing communication (and interaction).

2 – To explain, I shall resort to an example of "human pyramid" psychology[7] (i.e., anthropomorphism between people, rather

---

3 Such as the European macroeconomic boost encouraged by German reunification that had finally reached the vast world of craftsmanship and light industrialization in the deep South, or the encouragement given to my students in the province of Campania to look at what was actually happening "on their doorstep," or their "discovery" of numerous mini-activities that would become prime subjects of research for their "super-theses." Or the gradual emergence of a picture of the South that struck back against the despairing image of the Mezzogiorno (to put it mildly) that then prevailed in Italy and Europe. Or the opportunity, seized by Mario Pirani and some young journalists in his entourage, to sound the charge of "new orders, comrades," etc. (See *Italia Vulcanica*, 2018-22).

4 Here I am referring, of course, to the "American gravitation" of Nicoletta Stame and myself, the long collaboration with Albert O. Hirschman and the teaching of economic policy (see previous note) that "exploded" — in terms of student participation and cultural influence — in the mid-1990s. [On the latter experience, see also the first volume in this trilogy, *An Education*, ed. by N. Stame (2024)].

5 Such as the National Committee for the Emergence of Unregulated Labor, the South-North dialogue on democratic federalism, the International Colorni-Hirschman Institute and Entopan (now in full swing).

6 To use the expression of Piero Bassetti (2015) who also refers to the descendants of Italian emigrants and more generally to all those who appreciate and engage with Italian culture in its different aspects.

7 Which is not to be thought of, however, as a perfect geometric structure like the pyramid of Caius Cestius in Rome or of Giza in Cairo (to be clear). It is rather an immense mountain, tall and spiky, with numerous ravines and steep paths.

than with respect to nature, the stars or the universe).[8] It stems from a singular observation — that we live at different altitudes on a mountain, but a mountain which many of us wish were flat. It is a condition of abnormal *squinting*, in which we know full well that the world consist of stairs (which some go down and some go up), but we wish it did not. It thus happens that, mysteriously, a vertical view becomes horizontal. While the concrete economy verticalizes the world, economics, which is supposed to reflect it, follows a horizontalist approach....

[...] On February 17, 2021, President Draghi told the Italian Senate that "there is no Europe without Italy" (the senators applauded). Would he have ever said that there is no Europe without the Mezzogiorno, without Greece, or without Albania? I think not. Because his statement exposed, in the audience, the (unmentionable) desire for our country (or, more exactly, its Center-North) to be promoted into the "two engine [Germany and France] club."

On the one hand one recognizes (inevitably) the condition of relative subordination to the dominant peoples and powers, while on the other, one seeks to annul it, desiring a place in a kind of "exclusive partnership" — but among equal powers.

3 – The implicit analysis is verticalist, while the desire would be horizontalist — for us, of course, not for those peoples and those countries that follow us in the rankings. Indeed, often, the effort of relative ascent comes at the expense of others. Consider, for example, how European policies of (so-called) austerity have helped Germany rise *au dessus de la mêlée* — even to the detriment of Italy, which has meanwhile reduced its industrial production, lost several "national flagships" and has had to accentuate (*faute de mieux*) its "tourism focus"....

---

8 Colorni-Spinelli (2020), ch. 6.

5

Despite formal equality among different small and large EU countries, their substantive pyramid is characterized by continuous upward and/or downward adjustments reflecting internal and external relations of dominance-subordination that are in perpetual flux in the different dimensions of the real world. Often in such circumstances, minority conditions are used as a steppingstone by those who dominate them — to elevate themselves further. Once again, vertical-horizontal anthropomorphic squinting conquers the scene.

It must be added, however, that dependency relations, fortunately, sometimes undergo wide fluctuations. The dominant culture can change its mind about what to do and orchestrate a shift further down the pyramid. This was how in the postwar period the success of the Marshall Plan in Europe created the beneficial illusion that it was possible to trigger development in economically backward countries *ex abrupto*, and prompted the genesis of a sub-discipline — development economics — which subsequently "decayed," however, because of the disappointment that followed its entry into the field.[9]

In general, one must learn to act in different situations.[10] Always keep in mind the alternatives, the possible transition from one to the other, and even their co-presence at different levels of the pyramid.[11]

---

9 Hirschman (1981), Ch. 1. There has thus been a return to more traditional forms of economic thinking, to the point (to bring things home) that the reactionary policy of austerity inspired by unified Germany has deflated the EU as a whole (including Italy) and hit Greece hard. (And to think that Goethe wrote, among other things, "of all peoples, the Greeks have dreamed the dream of life in the most beautiful way" — now in Goethe, 2014, p, 96). But then the policy was partly rectified and now, in the midst of the pandemic and economic crisis, it seems to want to take new paths...

10 Even though — clearly — proceeding "unbridled" is generally more inviting to those operating in favor of the Colornian magnet because it allows more room to maneuver.

11 Like openings, yes, but conditioned by an austerity imposed further down, or vice versa as austerity at the top that actually allows "the mice to play," etc.

This, then, is the problem. There is, in my opinion, *a potential cause of the dependent world* that we need to be able to intercept and interpret intelligently, not least with the intention of convincing people, getting them on board, and progressively encouraging "everyone" to follow it.

To this end, it is necessary to set about the task of gradually mastering the area of the pyramid in which each individual is located, and knowing how to exploit the fluctuations of the policies pursued. In discussing this, I shall refer in the following pages to a specific experience, but it is clear that the examination of a number of events of various kinds will be necessary in order eventually to arrive at any useful conclusions.

4 – Yes, all right... – the prospective reader will think. But why Italy; why the Mezzogiorno?[12]

Of course, the rest of the planet can (indeed, must) also contribute to such an ambitious medium-to-long-term project. Yet it is clear, in my view, that in order to get a good sense of how things are, one has to "go down in scale," because that squint we mentioned also inhabits different countries (at the municipal, provincial, regional levels), and Italy and the Mezzogiorno (indeed the various Mezzogiornos) can provide, *inter alia*, a good point of observation (and starting point). That is to say — it (they) can be examined as "a case in point" within a much larger situation.

There are, of course, numerous intellectual manifestations

---

[12] The reason Italy can play a leading role in a universal process of civilization is something we all know. Its history and culture perennially carry this message to observers even in the remotest corners of the earth. Instead, why the Mezzogiorno can (and should) have such a function is something learned by doing — it concerns above all cultural and behavioral characteristics and potentials that are not obvious at first glance, but which have deep roots (deeper than Italy's, it could be argued) and which can really emerge through the enhancement of the great reservoir of Mediterranean people and things that still today remains largely unexpressed.

of all kinds (whether from a city, province or region) from the North that claim to represent our country (or even Europe) as a whole.[13]

And it is also true that many people talk about Italy referring to their own homes — while at the same time taking into account the preponderance of the North in every field. Thus, if they live in the Center-South they refer to the *Bel Paese* generally meaning "from here up" (and never down!). It is a statement that exposes the phenomenon of "automatic amputation" which in itself involves the daydream of being admitted to the club of prosperous regions.[14]

If, on the other hand, our compatriots live in the North-Central regions they usually follow the same procedure,[15] but implicitly[16] — in the sense that they prefer to elegantly overlook the rest of the country, not least so as not to fall into the unseemly elocution of Pius IX, commonly known to have considered the Mezzogiorno "the tail of Italy…"

In other words, the psychological antagonism I have spoken

---

13 It struck me as grotesque, considering their respective sizes, for example, that the lioness of Italy (Brescia) would claim to meet the Chinese dragon as an equal...
14 Or even to dominate them. Consider, for example, the recent "sanctification" of Maradona by the Neapolitan people. And writing this note calls another example to mind. At the presentation in the Campania hinterland of a volume of mine — *Milano-Napoli. Prove di dialogo federalista (Milan-Naples. Evidence of Federalist Dialogue* [2010]) — a man of a certain age (perhaps a teacher) stood up to say that he agreed with what he had heard, except for the title, because it should have been Naples-Milan, not Milan-Naples. Also, at the opposite end of the scale, I was reminded of a demonstration some time ago of women from Calabria hoisting signs that read, "We are Italian too!" (But is it possible, I thought, in the very land of the legendary King Italo, that these women were afraid of being shut out? Yes!) In my view, it is unwise to dismiss the thousands of episodes of this kind as mere parochial skirmishes. On the contrary, these are revealing mental attitudes of the human condition — exactly what I intend to question....
15 Like the many Emilians who think of their region as 'Lower Bavaria.'
16 Which shows up again and again at the governmental level (in Rome as in Brussels), especially in the technical-administrative structures that certainly have no desire to get their shoes dirty with southern assignments....

of elsewhere[17] reflects the pyramidal form of the economic-political structure.[18] Thus it would fall to the South (and the different Souths), especially in the beginning, to play the leading role. For it is only through the improvement of southern conditions (ours and others') that other parts of Italy and the planet may find an unambiguous role in the overall resurgence. To understand this, we need only imagine for a moment the consequences of an eventual accelerated development of the Mezzogiorno in the context of a revitalization of the Mediterranean.... Our capital would undoubtedly benefit greatly, and the North might also benefit in the European sphere. In other words, in the long-term interests of "everyone," we need to begin to gradually break out of the shell of the empires which, since the time of Alexander the Great (and Augustan Rome), have imposed all manner of Nessus shirts on Western humanity...

5 – But do we realize what this way of framing the issue would entail? It seems to me that we do not. Because the truth is, under the conditions we live in today, if we don't *dig in our heels* and consciously move against the tide, we will fall prey to the spontaneous workings of the market, and thus to its centripetal and centrifugal functions (of attraction and repulsion) that continually shape and reshape the space-time verticality discussed above.

Each pole tends to attract material and human resources generally greater than those it redistributes, an endless process

---

17 Starting with *Spendere Meglio* [Spending Better] (Meldolesi, 1992a), p. 76.

18 Hence yet another set of typical behaviors that can be observed with the naked eye. There are those who bind themselves to their small town, hunker down and accept fate ("cynical and cheating"); there are those who try to make a go of it locally; those who emigrate and focus on their children; those who commit themselves to school (or university) and then emigrate; those who have emigrated and look back with resentment; those who come back to scout around, etc. As I see it, these are all stories that, in one way or another, speak of the pyramidal hierarchies that tower above us...

that is accompanied, of course, by dominant political behavior (with a certain "hold" even over vast subordinate productive, social and political zones) — and which could be corrected (at least in part) by gradually creating alternative and competing poles.

In fact, it only takes a moment's reflection to realize that in the short term — it happens daily — each central and especially northern Italian area makes its own claims. Just as in the past, those in the North (Lombardy-Veneto first and foremost) may fall into the easy temptation to *oppose the South*.[19] How can we prevent that annoying refrain from coming around yet again?

It is indispensable to put down roots in Mezzogiorno. But it is clearly not enough to sympathize with the spontaneous resistance that arises, in a country as old as ours, to the day-to-day workings of the market, one must also work on developing the potential cultural and productive currents that run counter to it.

Here there is an actual litmus test at hand — the *willingness* of young people to engage in the empowerment of their land. For southern young people, this willingness is *far more significant* than what prevails among the young in other parts of the country.[20]

---

19 On the other hand, the readiness for change in the desired direction will gradually turn out to vary even within the Mezzogiorno, as a result of existing circumstances, social pressures and the way they develop.... For example, it is no accident, I think, that my students in the Neapolitan hinterland had in general greater readiness for change than those in the regional capital; or that, on balance, the region most responsive to our work was Calabria — as compared to the larger, more self-reliant ones (such as Campania, Puglia and Sicily) or smaller ones (such as Basilicata or Molise) to which, in the National Governing Body connecting southern Italian regions with the EU (Ministry of finance), we had initially turned for experience. See the eleven issues of *Italia Vulcanica*, 2018-21.

20 And I wonder, moreover, if this might not also be true of the East Germans vis-a-vis their counterparts in the West, for young people in less-developed parts of Europe and the Mediterranean in relation to those in more developed areas, and more generally for all the lands of the five continents that — deep in their hearts — feel the inescapable need to move up the ladder.

In addition, one must find the strength to get a move on. If everyone is looking up, towards the North, one could argue, it is well worth the effort to disobey and take a peek down. Not by chance, I was able to achieve real change when I convinced my students to observe what was going on right in front of their own homes.[21] I was unknowingly doing the groundwork for our boom.

Finally, it is imperative to reverse the direction of reasoning—in the sense that the direction of movement is no longer in imitating the top, but in valuing the bottom. Instead of elevating ourselves by pressing down on those below us, we need to turn around and give them a hand, so that we can progress together.

These are no doubt salient features worth reflecting on—step by step, in times of high tide as in times of ebb. It is a "common thread" that connects our experiences—those that have actually played out over time—and continue today, in thought and action, around a small pro-Meridionalist core.

6 - In this regard—as I explained in *Eppur si può!* [And yet, you can!] (2020a)—it is possible to evolve positively through the ups and downs and successive cycles of a world that oscillates and fluctuates—in communications, beliefs, cultures, propensities, etc.

Without doubt, our research on southern popular entrepreneurial tendencies set in motion an "operation truth" in (and concerning) the Mezzogiorno, which, however, created the illusion (only initially beneficial[22]) of the solution to southern development was within reach. So much so that, after a certain

---

[21] It is exactly in this way, in fact, that "the cloaked business" (copywrite Becattini) came into the open.

[22] Since it initially favors the mobilization of economic and social energy.

period, the initiative clashed with the historical accommodations, past and present, related to preexisting relations of domination/subordination.

It is worth briefly "unpacking" this point of view.

First of all, the fact that this was a truth operation (favored by circumstances) is not in dispute. It was our unequivocal "fact-finding" that opened the hearts and minds of those who, without prejudice, came into contact (through our very detailed field research) with the industrious swarm of southern small businesses and southern craftsmanship. Perhaps because they perceived the journalistic opportunity (of a blow-up!). Perhaps because such a vision eased collective anguish and helplessness in the face of such a key issue as the development of the South—which had seen so many policies founder for much of the postwar period. Perhaps because the ground was inadvertently prepared by the so-called "third Italy" (and its success).[23] Perhaps because the "findings" detected on the ground hinted at further possibilities...

On the other hand, it is also true that our initiative unintentionally created the illusion that a solution was at hand. Because black-white contrasts are an implicit fact in the journalistic game (lasting "the space of a morning"). Because no doubt there are at least two Souths in the South—but the point is that one is subordinate to the other.[24] Because those who got excited (including, briefly, Prodi, Ciampi, Treu, Scalfaro) generally knew very little about the South—and had not prepared

---

[23] In the sense that the reality of southern SMEs, while very different from that of the "third-Italy," was not (and is not) inconsistent with it, and hence becomes indirectly more understandable. [...] Yet, there is a small literature on the emergence of irregular SMEs in Emilia-Romagna and Veneto in the 1970s. Why prejudicially dismiss—some may have wondered—the possibility of a similar process occurring in the South?

[24] Such that its actual empowerment requires a vigorous, tortuous and complex emancipation process.

the necessary measures appropriate to the task.[25] And also because our activity, with its extensive resonance, had gradually awakened that broad circle (professional, financial, political, etc.) opposed to our ideas, which (from both the top and bottom of the pyramid) "brokered" domination of the South with its subordination—starting, of course, with the president of Istat... whose honor was wounded.[26]

And again because discussing rampant irregularity in the South somewhat resembled "talking about rope in the hanged man's house." In the sense that the formally regulated area of the South (which simultaneously may very well be clientelist, parasitical or corporate) felt (and feels) the instinctive need to keep away from irregularity,[27] and feared the "naked emperor" effect of the way things actually are... Instead, in the North they even went so far as to suggest, with good reason, that, yes, the Mezzogiorno should cure its social ailments—but went on to argue, at times, that the solution lay... in "throwing it overboard." But, seriously? Would someone do away with a sick sister or brother instead of nursing them to health? Unbelievable, *unacceptable*!

7 - On the other hand, while it is true that the "regularization issue" concerning southern business and labor has shown that it can be used as a lever—to gradually change what the country and the Mezzogiorno itself thought (and thinks) of itself, it is

---

[25] And beat a hasty retreat in the face of the explicit manifestation of the opposition.

[26] Meldolesi (1998a), ch.2, part two.

[27] The "limit" of this attitude was revealed to me at the Ministry of Labor when a senior official lost his patience and stated: "Professor, you have to stop talking about undeclared labor, because if we hear about it, we will be obliged to report it." It was undoubtedly a tell-tale incident revealing the large pocket of freeloading that has formed over time at the Ministry of Labor and in the (mostly southern) Job Centers, where employees simply refuse to deal with the main aspect of the problem—that of employment to be found and regularized—which, in theory, is what they are paid to do...

also true that, as in any upheaval, the "narrative" about the entrepreneurial potential of the South has had to contend, right out of the gate, with an ultra-unfavorable balance of power at the international, national, central and local levels.

And if, in spite of this, a stretch of road has nevertheless been traveled, an important role in this was undoubtedly played by Hirschman's lesson on development economics (along with the various fieldwork methodologies compatible with it). But the real protagonists were the students and recent graduates I met along the way. Their enthusiasm was decisive. They made it possible to bring the problem before the Italian people on the rising tide of their exuberant mobilization — which was both industrious and knowledgeable. These enterprising young people demonstrated with facts that their social condition could have its "golden moment,"[1] not least from an educational point of view (the time of their super-thesis and immediately post-graduation).[28]

The potential indeed exists. It is set in motion by the initiative of the stakeholders, based on a constellation of preexisting favorable circumstances that evolve over time. On a day to day basis, this collective opportunity may begin to manifest itself timidly — in an oscillatory pattern, and in successive waves. After going through a gradual phase of preparation "under cover," it can come to maturity, become visible, and erupt thunderously onto the scene through an unexpected surge which, upon reaching its apex, finally flexes and recedes. The 1995-98 trial represented the cusp of this kind of trend.

---

[28] The expression "the golden years" was coined by Franco Cioffi. Unfortunately, this positive predisposition did not produce a corresponding outcome, as happened, for example, in the experience with the National Governing Body connecting southern Italian regions with the EU. In fact, on this occasion the constellation of favorable circumstances fizzled. That is to say, the "friendly hand" that I intended to extend to those young people did not, at that juncture, encounter the governmental strength and determination that would have been necessary...

In such processes, what this great collective effort requires in the immediate term is to gain as much ground as possible — in terms of culture, publicity, influence, planning, and mindful action. In the final analysis — as I have repeated a thousand times — the only thing that counts is *the result*. It is this psychological drive that motivates our possibilism — the relentless, resourceful, sometimes daring search for proposals and exit routes appropriate to the purpose we are pursuing, which have to be put into concrete practice, right through to their actual implementation.

8 – But in such a process it is also useful to rack one's brains via medium- and long-term hypotheses and conjectures, in parallel with the actual experience as it unfolds and to get a sense of its further scope.[29]

Because at the outset, social movements allow one to envision the potential of the unfolding realities far into the future. If it is possible to put aside the illusory aspects of the issue, this allows for a less impressionistic idea of the adopted perspective.

Furthermore, collective movements have multiple consequences. The metaphor that always comes to mind is that of the stone thrown into the pond. Indeed, it so happens that despite the passage of time, we ourselves continue to feel the aftershocks of the "earthquake" of the 1960s-1970s. And not only — in its own small way, the Neapolitan high tide of the mid-1990s was undoubtedly affected as well.[30]

---

[29] As Alberto Carzaniga (2021) demonstrates in spades. It is the only one (that I know of) that proposes a reorganization of the state that starts with the resolution of some key problems of the Mezzogiorno. It is an inversion of the traditional North-South relationship that we should be able to re-propose — *pro domo nostra*.

[30] If only because the past has cautioned me in what I do (for better or worse, of course), in such a way that it has "piloted" my actions elsewhere — basing them on the record of experience and on a new Colorni-Hirschman apprenticeship.

2. MEZZOGIORNO, WITH JOY*

[...] We will start with a self-evident observation: when it is stated in the official forum that the South is "the least favored region" of the country, it is meant (obviously) that in the Mezzogiorno people do not live as well as elsewhere. This has an objective aspect — regularly documented by economic indicators — and a subjective one, and in fact the perception of the so-called "gap" is generally wider than what is recorded by quantitative data in both the southern and north-central regions. Spontaneous misinterpretations of its situation are profoundly divergent. In the South, there is a tendency to blame it on the North and the government, in the North on Southern society. It is very difficult — and perhaps not even useful — to assign blame and reasons for this. The question should instead be why we are faced with such peculiar, stubborn and entrenched collective psychological structures.

Activities and modes of behavior

Clearly our reasoning does not apply to the pleasant aspects of the Southern condition, the "beautiful day in Naples," or the almond blossoms of Agrigento. And on the other hand, in many ways, one cannot even speak of the Mezzogiorno as a homogeneous area. It is a group of regional societies differentiated internally, each of which is connected to the others more by culture handed down than by economic exchanges and interpersonal relations. But regarding the problem at hand, things are quite different. In every part of the South, albeit in a different form from area to area, one can easily see a further

---

* From Meldolesi, L. (2021 c), *Mezzogiorno con gioia!* Pp. 53-80. Originally published in *Nord e Sud* No. 2, 1990. The title echoes – in reversed – that of a well-known volume by Tibor Scitovsky: *The Joyless Economy*, 1976.

consequence of our opening observation. Relative depriva-
tion—in terms of per capita income, employment, civic services, as well as psychological—is reaffirmed every day by behavior that is sometimes chaotic, sometimes exasperating, and
which in any case diverges from what the development of the
South would call for. While its citizens are hardly aware of the
economic consequences of their daily actions, such actions
taken as a whole generate a less efficient collective rhythm of
life than in other parts of the country.[1] This is the classic dog
chasing its own tail—the lower degree of development corresponds to less productive behavior (and vice versa).

This would be a trivial observation if it were not so out of
step with the current way of thinking of economists.... As is
well known, political economy has generally assumed (for as
many as two centuries) the existence of standardized patterns
of human behavior, motivated by the pursuit of individual interest. And even development economics, which emerged in
the second postwar period to combat underdevelopment, has
often accepted the assumptions of the parent discipline. Thus,
with some exceptions, postwar Meridionalism, while motivated by political intentions, has generally steered clear of the

---

[1] At the same time there are major differences that (for reasons that will be
discussed below) are reflected in the collective consciousness. Thus, some areas of
the Marche and southern Lazio, although belonging to the initial territory
designated for the Intervento Straordinario, do not consider themselves to be in
the Mezzogiorno, while others, such as the Abruzzi and certain parts of Puglia,
tend to be labeled "Third Italy." (In this regard more can perhaps be said: along
with the North-South dialectic, the analysis of the Italian Mezzogiorno should take
into account—according to a thesis of Fernand Braudel's—the East-West division
that runs through it. The Spanish and Genoese civilization of the southern
Tyrrhenian coast has long dominated that of Venetian leanings on the Adriatic
side, althouth the latter seems today to be taking its revenge. See, for example, the
report "Mezzogiorno" published by *Mondo economico* on June 22, 1991. The policy
of liberalization and public support that we will discuss further on, stemming from
a "Tyrrhenian" observation, could also consolidate the advancement of the
Adriatic seaboard and thus activate the process of recovery of the South in the
successive stages that Giacomo Becattini and Alberto Quadrio Curzio speak of).

issues related to collective psychology that we are trying to focus on here. Yet, as difficult as these issues are from an analytical point of view, their study makes a transgression outside the traditional intellectual groove of economics imperative, if only to keep alive the hope of coming to grips with the issues on the table. This, then, is our Rhodus. Once we focus our attention on the relationship between economic activity and behavior, we *ipso facto* enter a no-man's land where it is difficult (if not dangerous) for many economists to follow. This is the only way in my view to explain the obvious oddity of so much of the publicity on the Mezzogiorno, where the data and economic reasoning are typically accompanied by some obscure hint of Southern "malaise." This is plainly an artificial separation of the economic and non-economic elements of that society—a mental structure that must gradually be called into question.[2]

In Italy's southern regions, as in any ancient civilization, there is a certain legitimate pride people feel in their way of life and traditions, and there is also a limited perception, only partly conscious, of collective *formae mentis*. At the same time, we hear in the rest of the country that the problem of the Mezzogiorno is a matter of mentality. Thus, if exorcism of any sort is deemed pointless, logic dictates that we move toward an essay in understanding that seeks to comprehend motivations and behaviors (avoiding as far as possible the conditioned opposition of exaltation and denigration). Moreover, the economic policy aims that we pursue here may shelter us (within certain limits) from a danger instinctively anticipated by many economists—we do not intend to embark on grand cultural discussions that perhaps seek some arcane *ultima ratio* of Southern backwardness.[3] Furthermore, in all modesty, our research is concerned with the

---

[2] Cf. Hirschman (1988).
[3] Fortunately, history has shown that development is possible at different degrees

mismatch or partial mismatch of certain behaviors of various social sectors with respect to the requirements of development — it concerns their motivations and the direct and indirect ways of changing them. The inspiration for the present work is by now obvious.[4] Those who know the Mezzogiorno know that there is no shortage of potential. Along with the massive flow of transfers that in various guises take the road South, there exist in this area great human and material resources, often scattered, hidden or badly utilized. At the same time, much of the South lives in a condition of precariousness and (in part) scarcity (with even more perceiving it as such), which constantly and repeatedly pressures the political system to ensure the maintenance and expansion of public spending in the most diverse directions. This occurs, moreover, even though such outlays do not effectively succeed in mobilizing local capacities and resources. Thus, if we intend to study the relationship that exists between public spending and productive forces, we must direct attention to aspects that are not in reality strictly economic.

To introduce the argument, I would like to recall a misgiving that has surfaced in recent years in the minds of several southern economics practitioners — what if this state spending were hurting the South? What if a kind of crowding-out were taking place such that the attraction exerted by public spending (through unproductive hiring, intricate "competitions" for orders and contracts, commissions... brokerage, etc.) were diverting some of the best entrepreneurial and professional resources away from profitable activities? What if, as FIME (Finanziaria

---

of latitude, in countries of different sizes, with or without natural resources, inhabited by more or less numerous populations, belonging to different races, religions, civilizations...

[4] Cf. in particular Hirschman (1958) (especially ch. 1 and pp. 138-139, 185-187) and Meldolesi, (1992b).

Meridionale) President Sandro Petriccione has long complained, the transfer of public funds directly to administrations and businesses systematically bypasses banks, alienating them from their job of selecting and supporting investments and relegating them instead to treasury and loan functions similar to those typical of real socialism? What if the practice (and expectation) of assistance were inducing a passive attitude at the mass level, almost an inverted reflection of the ancient tradition of nobility in the Mezzogiorno? What if this atmosphere of assisted job insecurity rewarded corruption and fostered an inclination to illegality among young people? These questions interest me, first and foremost, from the perspective of the economic and psychological returns on government spending.

Psychological antagonism

Let us try and frame the question more precisely. A high discrepancy between desired transformations and current behavior is typical of less developed societies. As a result of their internal movement and the attraction exerted on them by advanced countries, these societies everywhere express a will for economic and social improvement, but the motivations and conduct of different sectors of the population are inadequate to the purpose and lead to repeated disappointment. The great difficulty in development thus lies in learning by doing — that is, in gradually learning to adapt behavior to the demands of economic growth.

On the other hand, it is not necessarily the case that the behavior to be changed has traditional roots (which should in any case be interpreted going back to the hierarchical world of their formation): they are also the result of modern social interactions that, as such, may not be conducive to development. It is then a matter of understanding — again using the method of observation and induction—how these processes can originate, become collective psychological structures, and be protracted over time. To this end, I think it is useful to reflect (from below) on another typical characteristic of our country—its present rapid transformation. Hence, it is not uncommon to witness a "category jump" of a town or a province located at any degree of latitude. Due to intensified growth some inhabitants become aware, usually with some delay, that they are different—they are more productive, more organized, richer than their neighbors. This realization, often sharpened by their enthusiasm, provokes a change in their relative standing—they will feel that they have gained ground with respect to traditionally superior towns or provinces, and have now distanced themselves from their once comparable neighbors. Hence the emergence of an attitude of condescension toward the latter, along with the emergence of types of behavior more in keeping with their new status—in education, investment, risk-taking—that may in part legitimize their new position of leadership.

But others affected by relative change may be pushed toward opposite attitudes. Even if only to rein in the hubris of others, they will appeal to their own "social sense," setting some traditional forms of their own collective life against the "materialism" of their neighbors. And this may inadvertently contribute to forms of rigidity in their own behavior, including ones that would be better toned down for the sake of development. Thus, in this drama in a teacup, the emerging cities and provinces will tend to strengthen their relative advantage, while the backwardness of others may worsen.

Of course, this relationship is not deterministic, and indeed things may change again. The up-and-comers, having moved past the intoxication of success, may realize that they are actually not so different from the others, while the latter may put aside their resentment to make up lost ground. But, if the imbalance (for a complex of economic, historical, and political reasons) festers and drags on over time, the initial psychological antagonism is likely to silently solidify and leave its own deep imprint on the collective psychology, eventually turning into a cultural archetype.

Thus, the well-known modern and contemporary phenomenon of the spread of our country's economic growth from north to south has long created a kind of conditioned effect in the population. Each area generally tends to compare itself with those located further north in latitude ("from here up") and rarely with those further south. (Instinctively, the Milanese distance themselves from Romans just as Campanians or Pugliese do from Sicilians—and Sicilians themselves certainly do not wish to be taken for North Africans...).

In short, the concern not to sink, and if anything, to rise in latitude represents an unconscious yet vain national sport. The effect of psychological disruption and aggravation that is easy to perceive in the microcosm of relative change, qualified by regional peculiarities, reverberates in the thousand small-town quarrels of the Italian provinces. And it weighs especially on the gap between North and South because of a historical feature of major importance—the South has not known the kind of communal civic culture and social differentiation present in other parts of the country. Thus, the standardized nature of its culture, traditionally animated by a feeling of collective religiosity, also expresses itself in reverse in a general resentment toward the North.

Let us return then to our problem. Despite the great processes of change that have taken place in the South, and in spite of the substantial support offered by public transfers, the vast majority of Southerners think they are discriminated against. The existing material gap between themselves and other parts of the country is perceived as the product of an outrageous injustice. Hence the intense attitudes and behaviors, often a mixture of tradition and unscrupulous "availability," that fail to find the necessary developmental path. Hence again the sense of impotence that for long intervals seems to blanket entire areas and populations. Hence, finally, the pressure on the state, which from being a "Piedmontese" authority has turned in the postwar period into the only relief valve for a situation that is in many ways arcane and cannot be understood and changed. If we then look more closely into the Southern kaleidoscope, we see the picture fragmenting and recomposing itself into many ways. First, urbanization and the dormancy of traditional solidaristic elements have made for a poorly integrated society, where in everyday life individualistic and disruptive disputes clearly prevail over solidarity. The lack of trust in others creates a depressed atmosphere.[5] The economic opportunities that do exist are likely to be underestimated by local as well as domestic and foreign operators, many of whom are afraid to "get entangled" in the South.[6] Moreover, those who have fled the South are generally overwhelmed by the strain of the change (from the disruption suffered in their homeland of origin and the effort to integrate in their adopted homeland)

---

[5] Thus, a psychological vicious circle is formed. Lack of trust in the community opens the way for disruptive individualism which forces subjects to conform (or to go along, in the sense of complicity), thus producing even more distrust in the community. Hence the need to appeal to the state (or to blame it) as if the state alone, as an external authority, can break this spell people suffer from without understanding why.

[6] Even in the small world of the university, there is often a misperception of Southern reality. But experience teaches that the way to rectify this and turn it into analysis is by no means smooth. It is necessary, in my opinion, to live in the South but also outside the South, to link one's reasoning to the most convincing expressions of international economics and social science, to compare southern society with other areas (especially Southern Europe and Latin America), and to use contacts in the field – and also one's teaching work – to try and explore the starting hypotheses in depth and to test them relentlessly.

and fail to play the role of *trait-d'union* between the two situations. Finally, those who approach from the outside, if they are not infected by the desire to escape that dwells in the souls of many Southerners, are nevertheless still subject to an acceptance *sub conditione* – that is to say, to an initial favorable reception (even too favorable) that can turn into rejection, because, as they say in Sicily, they are still "from the continent."[7]

This sort of internal *pied-noirism* completes the picture of Southern psychological difficulties. An ancient society, buffeted by the winds of change, yet (in part) barred from the need for greater integration. A society that has voted massively in favor of a single Western European government but is struggling to find the pace of that vision. Is it not entitled to a deliberate economic policy capable of taking the measure of its complexity?

A daily tragedy

As is well known, in the 1950s-1960s Meridionalism reached important milestones of productive and social transformation, but while referencing various viewpoints, it generally set the problem of development in terms derived from growth theory (and thus related to the capital-output ratio, the investments deemed necessary, the new jobs that would be created, etc.). On the other hand, the contemporary Meridionalism that accompanied the transition from the Cassa per il Mezzogiorno to the Agenzia gave rise to some debate (on development alternatives, on the instruments of intervention), but it was unable to cope with the clientelist-welfare impulse that asserted itself in the

---

[7] This is clearly the exact opposite of what one might (reasonably) expect. It reflects an ambiguity of consciousness torn between the expectation of change and the (unconfessed) desire to preserve one's own rhythm of life. It thus happens that pinning one's expectations on those from the outside actually masks a hope for failure.

Mezzogiorno (especially) over the course of three decades.[8] While income has been increasingly sustained by subsidies, southern productivity problems have worsened, creating the sensation of a dismal drift in which public power reacts "spontaneously" (and in the usual forms) to electoral pressures; and in which entrepreneurial initiative, while showing signs of vitality, is in danger of remaining episodic.

So even after so much effort, a difficult situation has thus arisen, and the country seems powerless in the face of it. An emergency expenditure refinanced for another 24 trillion, a foreign exchange deficit of 60 trillion, a per capita output that is little more than half that of the North-Center, a state-dependent production structure that in large majority gravitates to the local market, a low rate of labor-force participation, a high level of demand for public and white-collar positions. These things are well known. But perhaps we have not given enough thought to the degree of social and political pollution that increasingly goes with them—especially in parts of Sicily, Calabria and Campania. Yet it is from these high-risk regions (to which I feel particularly attached[9]) that a non-ritualistic line of reasoning can take off.

Let us therefore change register and mentally focus on the criminal phenomenon infecting these societies—its expansive trend and its growing influence in various sectors of the population and economic activity. Our focus will be on the creeping delinquency organized around public procurement and local authorities, and on the overload of tasks and functions allocated to them by the Intervento Staordinario and formalist

---

[8] 1975-1990

[9] Also, because, despite being from a Veneto-Tuscan (and *"buzzurra"*) family, circumstances of life led me to work in Sicily, Calabria and Campania. (The term *"buzzurro"* was used by Romans to describe the officials and professionals who settled in Rome after the unification of Italy, because they ate well, and had *"la buzza,"* the belly).

legislation that indirectly favors corruption (to "expedite" paperwork) and the intrusion of criminality (to obtain permits, contracts, etc.). Let us focus on the use being made of our democracy at the grassroots level, on local politicians smelling of corruption, on their conniving and quarreling with their patrons, and on levels higher up, until a disturbing shadow creeps to the top.

It is clear, first of all, that the country should do much more to treat its diseased wing—not so much in terms of resources, but in terms of attention and the ability to step in. How to improve administration, education, health, the environment and so many other things in the affected regions? How to discourage illicit activity and encourage public interest in its different forms? This is where we come to the point. Faced with the worsening daily tragedy, the economist, touched at close quarters, might finally break out of his or her mental patterns and think the unthinkable (or what at first glance would appear to be so).[10]

What then does the Mezzogiorno need? My answer is that, even prior to any new actions, the South needs a policy of liberalization that would gradually eliminate its status as a separate zone or as a country within a country—a policy that pushes companies, institutions and individual citizens toward conduct more in keeping with the workings of the single European market they intend to enter. It needs a policy of deregulation, reduction of state presence in the economy, of financial inter-mediation and the automatism of public intervention.

---

[10] It is not easy to reach this conclusion from the inside, not least because of the different level of social pollution people live in—if one is not affected personally there is still hope that the criminal phenomenon may recede back to its traditional trafficking, that the threshold of clientelism may come down, and that collective life can resume a rhythm that is at least bearable. But all this evaporates (and can trigger panic) when the phenomenon approaches and exceeds a certain vital threshold.

Instead of an increasingly intricate body of special legislation, what is needed is drastic simplification and progressive deregulation. In the place of a hyper-present state, a public dimension and public responsibilities need to be re-established that are compatible with those of other Italian and European regions (in terms of employment, functions, efficiency, transfers, etc.). Instead of marginalizing credit activity, the Southern banking-financial system should be strengthened and induced to support industrialization. Rather than relentlessly fueling traditional political-administrative channels with their network of patronage (and related extortion), the path of automatism should be taken, which would remove a lot of *de facto* (rather than *de jure*) discretion from the authorities in charge.[11] I would like to stress this last point. With the growth of corruption and the infiltration of the underworld into local governments, the elimination of some areas of de facto discretionary administration has become more urgent than ever. A study is needed of an automatic system for the flow of public money so as to create, on this front as well, a supportive floor that economic actors (southern and otherwise) can walk on unhindered — i.e., without having to engage in the exasperating search for *entrée* and "bargaining." (To get an idea — this involves producing a change in many ways analogous to what happens to the temptation to evade taxes when a self-employed worker becomes a wage earner with automatic withholding).[12]

---

[11] Despite appearances this viewpoint is not at odds with the push for decentralization proposed in many quarters. On the contrary, the reduction of functions and the de facto discretionary latitude attached to them would allow a progressive remission of current centralism and would thus be essential to enable a parallel increase in local accountability and grassroots democracy, which works very poorly today. It could also be linked to a process of devolution of functions.

[12] To begin the discussion I would suggest considering the following points: factoring in the automatic supports that already exist (such as collecting highway tolls); effective collection of payment for services we turn a blind eye to [.] through

In this way it would be a liberal and progressive turning point for inducing economic actors to engage with the market and gradually recover from a serious symptom of clientelist welfarism (and real socialism)—lack of confidence in one's own strengths. It is a turnaround which, accompanied by public policy, would assist a series of movements that already exist in the Mezzogiorno—produced indirectly by industrial re-conversion, cultural growth, productive decentralization, returning emigrants, etc. Moreover, it could attract new Italian and foreign capital to the South and propel Southern entrepreneurship to the forefront, not least to change *in loco* the political and social balances.[13]

On the other hand, to understand the lesson one need only reflect on the fact that even a few hundred kilometers away, populations with similar cultural traditions have very different patterns of behavior. Those who work in the (so-called) "Third Italy" have been inspired to believe in the concrete possibility

---

automatic penalties on authorities in default; possible support for the Southern economy with somewhat lower prices of some services (gas, electricity, public transport) instead of through granting various gratuities; the possibility of a lower tax burden (direct and indirect) accompanied, however, by a much more targeted, intelligent and automatic effort to prevent evasion. Moreover, with regard to the vast field of permits, incentives, procurement, etc., it will be necessary to guard against apparent automatisms that actually conceal their opposite (e.g., regarding capital grants, see Galli and Onado, 1990, pp. 19-24). Instead, it would be necessary to survey this discretionary area, reduce it in breadth and increase its responsibility, directing it toward a higher return on expenditure and subjecting it to intensive auditing and reforms that would enable it to carry out vigorous rehabilitation (see below).

[13] According to many Southern entrepreneurs—as we often read in business newspapers—success is not due to public support—it occurs in spite of it. Of course I have a hard time imagining that successful entrepreneurs in the Mezzogiorno have done without the tax exemptions or incentives provided by the law. Rather, I think their statements—for the spontaneous and truthful elements they undoubtedly contain—are a testimony to the need to "do it yourself," if only so as not to be overwhelmed by the sliminess of client relationships. Not surprisingly, there is noticeable intolerance among entrepreneurs in the Mezzogiorno toward the political class, and this could turn into support for indirect forms of public support such as those mentioned in notes, 12 and 21.

of an improvement in their conditions through work: the experience itself activates the feedback loop of work, increased productivity, income, and consumption. On the contrary, those who are most committed to work of any kind in the South often have to fight the idea, typical of the patronage-welfare system, that working is for chumps, that it is connections that count, para-social pressures (if not *omertà*, corruption, easy money). The change of climate that one can experience even on the same day traveling by car from one region to another is inescapably obvious to the objective observer—only true deregulation can offer breathing space (psychological space included) to Southern entrepreneurial forces, especially the small and medium-sized companies which the restoration of the social and productive structure typically depends on.

This gives rise to an important research question. There has been in the South what seems to be an unstoppable decline in traditional trades—agricultural, craft oriented, maritime—and with them an entire world, a collective mentality, is disappearing. (In local parlance, "travail" and "toil" have now taken on a negative connotation.) But the process of transition to modern motivations and behavior has had great difficulty in taking hold. It would be valuable to document the different stages of consciousness—interregnum conditions, disturbing and devastating tendencies—and the positive embryonic forms that need in any case to be directly or indirectly stimulated so as to strengthen and quicken the pace of emancipation.

And Europe?

I would like to elaborate on the thinking behind the formation of the European single market. Among insiders, the concern that immediately came up had to do with the effects—overwhelmingly negative—that the fateful year 1993 might produce on the productive structure of the Mezzogiorno. The emphasis has been on constraints (related to financial and fiscal incentives and specific investments) rather than on the possibility that a closer link with the European locomotive might represent an opportunity to emerge from its own doldrums. Shouldn't the beneficial logic of European federalism also be felt in the "southern zone" of the continent?

Soon, one might reason, since the problems of the Mezzogiorno will have to find a place within the Community's regional policy, we might as well start observing them already from this point of view — for example, with reference to the "Optimum Currency Area."[14]

Three conclusions can be drawn from this traditionally constructed theory (which might easily be translated into other languages as well). Firstly, the formation of an "optimal monetary area" conducive to the development of all regions within it, requires real wage flexibility that reflects differences in productivity. In addition, inputs must be flexible to allow their reallocation in order to correct emerging imbalances and to achieve the highest possible efficiency in the whole area. And mechanisms must exist for "automatic" transfers between the regions concerned. The comparison between these recommendations, the formation of the single market and the policies of assistance followed in the Italian South have fostered the emergence of a new literature.[15] My impression is that such a viewpoint, with the

---

[14] This is an outlook originally advanced by Tibor Scitovsky (1958, cf. especially ch. 2: "Balance of payments theory and the problem of a common European currency"). It was later taken up and refined by Robert Mundell and Ronald McKinnon in two communications published in *The American Economic Review* (September 1961 and September 1963).

[15] Cf. Sarcinelli (1989); Padoa-Schioppa (1988a and 1988b); Galli and Onado (1990). The latter takes the coming single market deadlines as a starting point for a survey of the real and financial aspects of the Southern economy and a critique of some of the policies followed thus far. The essay notes that if it had performed as well as the Center-North, capital accumulation in the Mezzogiorno would have generated a much higher total output. To explain this difference, it focuses in particular on interest and (especially) capital subsidies. It shows that the non-

support it will be able to rally in national and community circles, will likely have a positive influence — provided, however, that it is worked out in close contact with the concerns of the Mezzogiorno and is supplemented by further propositions.

First, when we shift the starting point of the "Optimum Currency Area" to the level of recommendations, the reasoning may become entangled. The root cause is that economists, taking their model as a starting point, implicitly suggest the primacy of the relationships analyzed here at the expense of other aspects (institutional, social, psychological, etc.). Thus, following economic logic, it would seem that the first of the theory's three recommendations is the central one — it could be argued that if wages are flexible worker mobility will inevitably occur, and that automatic intervention can serve as a corrective at the level of equity. My idea is that in a sense the reasoning should be reversed. Let us return to economics and its problems with collective psychology. It is well known that labor market mobility in the South is highest at the top of the employment pyramid, while it is significantly reduced in the middle and lower ranges.[16] Word has it that it pays to move

repayable subsidies in current legislation imply a very low, if not negative, investment discount rate. "One might ask," the two authors write (pp. 21-22), "whether such low interest rates do not alter the quality of the projects. Do they not shift the terrain of competitive confrontation from the market for goods to the relationship with the bank and the public administration; do they not make investment in human capital aimed at obtaining state subsidies more cost-effective than investment aimed at improving business efficiency?"

[16] Alongside differences concerning the tasks performed, this pyramidal observation requires the identification of some differences in economic-social placement. Among salaried employees I would distinguish, for example, between public employees, whom today's *vox populi* points to as privileged employees with guaranteed stability, employees of companies with little or no unionization, marginal employees, and precarious day laborers (who often cannot afford to be unemployed). And in the inactive population I would distinguish between unemployed people who are looking for a good job, those who can afford to be unemployed (living on the backs of parents, spouses, etc.), unemployed people in need, and marginalized people living on public or private assistance. The rationale for these "rungs" is to get closer to how things actually are and to study people's needs and potentials concretely. One

only for a good position, otherwise it is better to stay with the family, get by with an illegal job (from 600-700,000 lire a month) and sign up on the "lists" (of the employment office, the organized unemployed, the politician 'who can,' the school, etc.,). This leaves open several thankless occupations — from domestic service to heavy labor, to very small time trade—where workers of color flock. On the other hand, union and client pressure to get a position is really a demand for income rather than work, so that growth in public employment does not ensure a corresponding increase in related services. What increases is mainly inactivity... in lieu of moonlighting.

Fortunately, there is also a reverse side of the coin. When, as a result of the public deficit, the government decided on a freeze on permanent hiring, something curious happened in a small municipality in the Naples area. Since municipal hiring now concerned specific jobs and was for a fixed term (three months), it was not worthwhile for many to leave their off-the-books jobs — so that the unemployment rate recorded by the employment office suddenly plummeted. This episode (along with many others that could be cited, positive and negative)[17] comforted me with the idea that the liberalization policy mentioned

---

need only begin this exercise to realize that the common attitude of blindly "trusting" the ISTAT (National Institute of Statistics) unemployment rate is misleading. It does not include all the unemployed. It does not distinguish between the different conditions and intentions of people who are not working. And it does not emphasize the functioning of the market — that is, the correspondence (higher or lower) of the respective composition of labor supply and demand in different parts of the country.
[17] It is well known, for example, that in Campania, the unwillingness to accept "socially useful work" (ex-Article 23 of the 1988 Finance Act) has climbed past 40%. (Moreover, we have no way of knowing how much weight was given, in the decision of those who declared themselves "available for work," to the scarcity of work commitments that would leave room for other activities — such as being a student — to be done concurrently and would also offer the hope of climbing a step toward a stable position). Cf., finally, the results of the research on nearly two thousand young people registered on the employment rolls in eight cities of southern Italy promoted by the Agnelli Foundation and coordinated by Mariano D'Antonio (1991).

above would not only have an important direct effect — compatibility and legal certainty, discouraging free-riding, corruption and economic crime — its consequences would also be indirect and more far-reaching. Among other things, if accompanied by an expansion of the market economy, it could play a decisive role in (inadvertently) fluidizing the Southern labor market — as is the case (according to a well-known interpretation) with the thronging of the Beguines for the blood of San Gennaro.

In essence, liberalization could profoundly alter expectations, leading individuals to consistently increase the quality, quantity and range of the jobs they are willing to perform in exchange for a good starting salary (over a million liras). And it is easy to see that the "comparative advantage" of the South, compared to other European areas would be positively affected.[18]

(Finally, I consider the issue of wage differential — which is certainly not an impassable line — as internal to such a process of change. This in the sense that the success of a liberalization policy, together with the gradual attenuation of the welfare and client system could bring with it a tapering-off of corporate unionism allowing the development of a waiting or tunnel effect.[19] This would encourage some tolerance of limited de facto wage gaps.[20] On the other hand, it seems to me difficult

---

[18] This process of interaction would be complementary to the classical view that initiation into industrial labor has positive indirect consequences for the functioning of society (Hirschman 1958, ch. 8). It would also alter the reality of emigration by reopening its channel in both directions. Of course, an eventual reactivation of the Southern labor market could be accompanied by housing, personal credit and training policies in order to stimulate occupational, sectoral and territorial mobility.

[19] Cf. Hirschman (1973)

[20] But it is also true that the special attention various economists give to the level of Southern wages may carry with it a number of meanings. In addition to the professional aspect alluded to, I make no secret of the fact that there may be a temptation to cut corners on lengthy surveys in the field in the hope of being able to simplify things, and perhaps even, beyond the controversy over bad governance, a certain desire for "normalization." I think, first, that we need to de-mythologize the meaning of the aggregate level of Southern wages. It refers only to the official sector of the

to proceed the other way around and to think of forcing a wage differential on the current system, for example through the reactivation of the famous wage cages: this would risk of stirring up processes of resentment amplified by the psychological antagonism discussed above).

Intervention and psychology

From all this, one begins to get a sense of how it is in the highest interest of the Mezzogiorno to "join Europe" — to set out without qualms on the road to liberalization, reap the economic and financial stimuli of the single market, and compete with other areas of the Community in welcoming new investments from Europe, America, Japan. Of course, this has to take place within a process of European integration that is beneficial for the whole country. Nevertheless, I would insist, a courageous policy of deregulation, privatization, financial mediation and automation is also essential in order to activate new credible policy initiatives in the Mezzogiorno.

In the first place, the policy of liberalization and the reorientation of production and employment proposed here would be implemented in a dynamic context, such that it would allow for incremental steps on the road to development, as concrete developmental opportunities were created in the South. The

---

economy, and, because of its specific characteristics, this distorts the comparison of the South with the rest of the country in two ways — on the one hand the official sector is more "public" in composition and on the other hand it is relatively less extensive in the South (as compared to the unofficial sector). Moreover, it is not fair to focus only on wages when discussing comparative advantages between different parts of the country. This is because investment decisions depend on many factors such as external economies (and dis-economies), industrial interrelationships, distances to markets, services, and public policy — not to mention, of course, the (often distrustful) psychology of investors. But, having said that, it seems right to shift the attention to the world of work. Not, of course, to cast aspersions on unions or workers, but to try to convince them that the state's clientelist hyper-presence, lack of accountability, "slackness" in labor, and corporate vindictiveness are real (and not just presumed) enemies.

success of the operation would lie in its ability to activate expansion through the liberation of market forces, so that economic actors would concretely feel the advantage of "joining Europe" and would aim toward phasing in the change regarding the (economic and social) situation and using the public resources available for development purposes *cum grano salis*.[21]

Clearly, this latter aspect has great significance. Not only because the new intervention will have to further oppose the old welfare and client system, but because at the psychological level it will also have to provide clear and lasting indications of rehabilitation to overcome the participants' initial reluctance.[22] There is a perception in the country today that money spent in the South scatters in a thousand rivulets, like in St. Patrick's well. This is magnified by psychological antagonism — in the North it is transformed *sic et simpliciter* into calls for drastic cuts, in the South into calls for better apportionment (not least to avoid "the usual split"). The risk, of course, is that initiatives that are unimpeachable from every point of view and which, it must be pointed out to the incredulous reader, really do exist, will be swept away with summary procedures, instead of being accorded value.

Unfortunately, interest in accumulating experiences with

---

[21] Although the following reasoning refers mainly to development projects, the problem of the productive and psychological effects of public intervention concerns other aspects of Meridionalist economic policy as well. Thus, in the case of current incentives (and their "consequences"), tax relief on profits might be considered, which would combine automatism (see, n. 12) with greater pursuit of profit (Giannola). Instead of the administrative (and clientelist) mentality that financial transfers generate in the Southern banking system, forms of subsidized loans could provide for a bank's co-participation in the investment risk (Galli). And instead of assistance to young people (however disguised) one might envision "honor credits".
[22] Mention was made above of the likely underestimation of Southern opportunities. Overcoming this lack of confidence to the point of triggering an 'avalanche' of foreign capital (as is occurring in Andalusia) is certainly a matter of paramount importance, but it is also unimaginable that it would not achieve concrete results on the crime issue and the economic liberalization front.

one's papers all in order (on a formal and substantive level) is more the exception than the rule. There is an understandable attraction to "winning" and spending new public funds, but there is no comparable interest in their performance — that is, in timely verification of how they have been spent and how they could be spent better. Efforts here seems to me insufficient at all levels, including inside the Department for the Mezzogiorno and the Investment and Employment Fund, which limit their work (to a large extent) to (*ex ante*) control of expected costs and benefits.[23]

This is a central problem. If it is not gradually resolved, any intervention project in the Mezzogiorno, no matter how well thought out, risks reviving the well-known social-political machine that has brought us from the "cathedrals in the desert" to the "crater." My view is therefore that it should be approached in a practical way, developing the rationale of evaluation to its full potential, "complicating" cost-benefit analysis and drawing on international experience. Here I would like to add that the reevaluation of public spending must be framed in a more general dimension.

To clarify this point, let us take up the reasoning of the "Optimum Currency Area." The same Scitovsky who, as noted, is at the origin of this conception later created a more complex line of thinking. To come to grips with the contradiction between economic theory and the great youth movement of the 1960s he reversed a long tendency to steer economics away from its psychological assumptions, reconnecting it instead to modern motivational psychology. Applying this to the US, he wrote *The Joyless Economy*.[24] I must confess that this

---

[23] Cf. Meldolesi (1992 a), ch. 3.

[24] Scitovsky (1976). This "inquiry into human satisfaction and consumer dissatisfaction" challenges the postulate of consumer theory to the effect that most consumers know what gives them satisfaction. Through motivational psychology it

book encouraged my own desire to press theory into reckoning with the psychology that prevails in the South, not in order to reveal disappointment (or depression), but the contrary — to gradually uncover the boldness and, I would like to say, the joy of possible change.

On the other hand, it does not seem to me that the Italian South can be simply homogenized to a pattern of market functioning as part of an "optimal currency area."[25] Rather, I think that while keeping the lessons of economics in mind, the development of the Mezzogiorno needs to be set in the context of a thorough examination of its problems, and carefully vetted initiatives (on the productive, social and psychological levels) need to be activated accordingly as a complement to the liberalization policy, so as to gradually orient the economic system toward the desired goals.

First and foremost, the proposed measures should trigger inducement mechanisms of various kinds, capable of attracting and employing (even indirectly) the many skills and resources present in the South — entrepreneurial and professional, technical, clerical, and manual skills, along with natural and tourist resources, capital goods, potential savings, etc. — along with many others from northern Italy and abroad. In addition, these projects would need to undergo systematic evaluation to monitor their actual results and at the same time fine-tune their operation. This is indispensable with respect to the capacities and resources actually utilized, the results achieved

---

instead analyzes different sources of satisfaction and concludes that many people do not know enough about what life and the market can offer them. (The importance of Scitovsky's endeavor probably transcends his own findings: cf., Hirschman 1982).

[25] Among other things, this could perpetuate its status as an aspirant to emancipation. In fact, because of its "permissive" nature (cf. Hirschman 1958, pp. 194-195) there is this risk in focusing solely on infrastructure. Cf. also the critique of Sarcinelli (1989) who recalls how, as early as the late 1950s, it was felt necessary to couple such a policy with an industrial policy.

(productive and environmental) and the effects produced on the lives and behavior of citizens.

This last aspect needs clarification, especially in terms of what we referred to above as the psychological performance of public spending—a concept whose negative aspect lies at the root of the liberalization proposal. As for its positive side, suppose, for example, that a well-constructed and verified policy intervention increases the number of community projects or the actual amount of work done. This would set in motion a psychological process of "cognitive dissonance," in the sense that subjects, accustomed to determined motivations and behaviors, would initially find themselves hesitant in the face of new opportunities, but would soon be drawn into engaging in activities at variance with their original routines. From here, their need to reduce such dissonance would then bring about a gradual change in behavior and (later) motivation—a reorganization of their lives and attitudes that could eventually result in a lasting readjustment.[26] Whether we look at it from this positive angle or from the negative angle (from the loss of habitual reliance on assistance, patronage, etc.), our reasoning ultimately aims to activate this process of reversing the relationship between thought and action.

It is thus clear that development does not consist of a mere increase in output—it induces processes of change and rethinking in the social fabric. Moreover, an increase in production that has occurred through differing pathways or sectors can have different psychological effects. Thus, a given intervention in the economy may lead subjects to think that the job (and its remuneration) is linked to either merit or opportunism; it may induce (even indirectly) subjects to change jobs, open a workshop or start a company; it may discourage illegality or encourage it, etc.

---

[26] Cf. Festinger (1957); and Hirschman (1965).

Mentally, these (and other) alternatives must always be kept "switched on," because "the art of promoting development may therefore consist primarily in multiplying the opportunities to engage in these dissonance-arousing actions and in inducing an initial commitment to them."[27]

To better understand this important point, let's take a step back and look again at the disruptive individualism that snakes through the Mezzogiorno. There are a number of typical symptoms of this, such as the reluctance of private individuals to invest for the long term, the search for the lucky break, the mindset of making "suckers" of others, the sometimes-sketchy compliance with business practices, and the high level of non-performing bank loans. And again, on a broader level, one can cite the preference for the hot niche, the need for conspicuous consumption, the pressure to mind one's own business, the chaotic traffic flow, the sloppy street cleaning (which contrasts with the spotless homes), the lack of respect for the functions and property of the state, etc.

Of course, this climate does not exclude the simultaneous existence of individual and collective solidarity processes — from the emotion created by some news item to a sudden onset of protest against drugs, kidnapping, racketeering, or the mafia. But protest generally arises when people are closely affected, and it is often temporary — so that it leaves the field to individualistic and disruptive normality. What is lacking, first and foremost, is sufficient confidence in the individual and collective ability to create adequate living conditions and prospects.

Now, it is only through practical action that different actors can be persuaded by degrees to gain confidence in their community (and themselves), and it is change that gives substance to that process. For this reason, as we study new forms

---

[27] Hirschman (1971), p. 325.

of action typically based on mechanisms of inducement, we must not lose sight of the fact that their aim (ultimately) is to modify behavior. Whether we are talking about unbalanced development or reversed sequences, about upstream or downstream linkages (or consumption, fiscal, capacity, or cultural linkages), about studying current or potential comparative advantages (of products now imported), about getting the labor force accustomed to industrial activity via the pace of the machinery, or about fostering the spread of development and curbing centralizing tendencies[28] — the problem that remains in each of these cases (and others as well) is understanding whether and how, from within a framework of progressive liberalization, the policies proposed to correct the spontaneous evolution of the economy can enhance its development and at the same time modify the behavior of economic actors in the desired direction. The latter objective, precisely because it would cause lasting change in the Southern condition, is clearly of the greatest importance.[29]

Postscript

The bottom line of this chapter — encouraging, I hope — is that the Mezzogiorno is not incomprehensible, nor is it unalterable — as claimed by those who assert with a sense of despair (perhaps spreading their arms), that "There is nothing to be

---

[28] Of course, I am referring here to chapters 3-10 of Hirschman (1958). To these must be added the recent idea (Hirschman 1990) that inducement sequences need to be assisted (and corrected) by elements of simultaneity in order to avoid the emergence of unwanted side effects. In certain cases, therefore, it is necessary to keep two things going at the same time, in a sense, to yield the formation of psychological structures commensurate with the society to be built — a democratic, market-based society, at once based on individual initiative and efficient collective solidarity.

[29] This obviously does not mean asking Southerners to abandon their cultural roots, but rather to rediscover them, bringing them into line with the more modern and civilized way of life they aspire to. In practice, it is likely that some characteristics will already prove compatible, others may be "circumvented" by development, others (against all expectations) will turn out to be favorable, and others finally will be modified.

done!"

To be sure, the South has many problems—from the behavioral enfranchisement of the population to the formation of a real leadership class (after the still recent dissolution of the Old Regime), to the upsurge of crime. But in our time the path to progress is not barred, provided of course that we can get a glimpse of it.

To that end, I have used a method of "*trompe l'oeil*"[30]—I have tried to lay out the argument of the present work in the simplest and most reasonable way, creating the optical illusion that the resulting economic policy proposals can be put into practice without problems. This intentional naivete is meant to delimit and further explore economic policy proposals—not for the sake of mere criticism, but to achieve an independence of judgment by which to evaluate things and perhaps embark on a new adventure that explicitly addresses the issue of putting the results achieved into practice. Thus, I am by no means hiding the resistance that a policy of liberalization may encounter in the Mezzogiorno, nor the difficulties of putting in place new forms of intervention. To get an idea of this, it is sufficient to recall that any large-scale project typically entails the opening of construction sites for several years and the temporary creation of jobs (and the related hope that they may become stable, perhaps at the expense of the state). It also mobilizes a whole environment of accountants, construction contractors, speculators, and fixers—not to mention, of course, multiplier effects. It is easy to see how large projects have a strong pull for political and union leaders, and how politicians in different areas are often evaluated based on their ability to "unlock funding." But the desired object is income, not long-term productivity, so that the mechanism in question does not

---

[30] Hirschman (1971), p. 29

ensure the proper use of the money invested, while it lends itself to being polluted by the "kickback economy" (as Mario Pirani called it) and even by organized crime. Politicians will try to reactivate it, at more or less regular intervals, in order to take advantage of the consensus and funding surrounding it.

However, with its tireless repetition, this "ideal type" (unfortunately concrete) of public spending can cause us to lose sight of the very possibility of change. By contrast, suppose then that at some point in our story it is possible to launch an anti-parasitic (and anti-criminal) counteroffensive that starts in one or more areas and succeeds in spreading to others. Suppose — to bring in some elements of our reasoning — that a real turnaround in law-and-order policy were achieved, that discretionary spending were significantly scaled down, that indirect automatism in favor of the South was strengthened, and that effective liberalization was developed. Would not the most positive forces in the South feel encouraged and gradually shift their weight to the right side of the scale?

Criminal metastasis feeds on other people's private and public wealth and at the same time destroys its foundations. This means that if all the forces (economic, cultural, religious, etc.) that are — or could be — its victims could be leveraged to reverse its expansive tendency, it would represent a real advance toward economic and social rehabilitation. This is a problem of the South, but not only. As this kind of criminality moves up the peninsula and builds important outposts in Lazio, in Tuscany, in Liguria and especially in Milan, the alarm becomes general — the important thing is to know how to turn it into a conscious, determined, prolonged counteroffensive.

Therefore I would like to conclude that in a world that is coming more and more within reach (because of shrinking distances, the democratic revolution in the East, the arrival of so many foreign workers), in a world in which our country —

much more than we realize—is now within a European construction where the different regions of the continent will have to coexist peacefully on the basis of competition, respect and mutual appreciation, one cannot help but be hopeful that the Italians of the North and those of the South eventually become aware of the psychological mechanisms that divide them.

The whole country—who can doubt it?—needs to get rid of criminality and parasitism, to strengthen democracy, to restore development. "The South," Judge Falcone argued, "needs the whole country at its side." And finally, I would like to add, it needs to rediscover in practice pride and confidence in its great geographical, material and human resources.

3. THE MEZZOGIORNO AND EAST GERMANY[*]

As always, the problem is to gain an understanding using the available data and information — to understand by actually going and seeing; by getting your shoes dirty, as Manlio Rossi-Doria used to say, studying given situations and comparing them with others.

The Mezzogiorno feels "bottled up" in an almost unique relationship with Northern Italy.[1] Growing integration generates a two-speed life in the South — the one allowed by Southern daily life, and the other pertaining to the "Northern" level of consumption (and thus income) that Southerners seek to emulate. When they return home, emigrants naturally bring news. But this does not alter the life of a settled population that gravitates around its municipality and suffers from economic asymmetries and psychological antagonisms. Hence the need to break the shell, to open channels in multiple directions, near and far, to head where the "return" (for the South) seems highest. To this end, I myself have practiced a little international to-and-fro over the years, consisting of travel, sojourns, research, university ties, etc., often following in the footsteps of Albert Hirschman.

For example, the "pivot" hypothesis between the North and South of Italy suggests comparisons between developed and developing countries — the United States, France and Germany

---

[*] From Meldolesi, L. (2000), *Occupazione e emersione*, pp.31-58.

[1] In *Le immagini del Mezzogiorno* [Images of the Mezzogiorno] (1999) Gabriella Gribaudi convincingly showed how the very idea of the Mezzogiorno and later its identity were shaped in the asymmetrical dialogue with the North of the country. Hence a twofold need arises. On the one hand, we must divest ourselves of what are frequently offensive formulations by rediscovering the independent realities and concerns of the South. On the other, we need to understand the concrete features, however limited, that are contained in such images (as Paolo Pezzino does, for example, in *Il paradiso abitato dai diavoli* [Paradise Inhabited by Devils], 1992), in order to correct and move beyond them to the point of defeating the internal logic of the disparaging attitude that produced them.

on the one hand, and Mediterranean countries, former socialist countries and Latin America on the other are obvious candidates. The intention is not so much to construct full-blown comparisons based on a whole range of elements. The complexity of human societies is such that I have found it useful to "temper" this approach with one of anthropological origin that suggests understanding others to interpret oneself.

In a sense, this is its "double." Indeed, as sociology tells us, to compare two realities one must have a common basis so that their differences can be clarified as variations on the theme. Anthropology, on the other hand, suggests looking first at extreme differences — between primitive communities and our industrialized societies — because it is their dissimilarity that initially triggers surprise in our minds and then an understanding of social aspects close to us that we had not understood. This is fine, one might observe, but how should one proceed in situations that do not lend themselves to either approach? My proposal is to use both, taking advantage of convergences (however limited) on the one hand and divergences (however extensive) on the other. That way we acquire higher margins of research freedom. The exercise is endlessly renewed because it addresses multiple issues and because societies are constantly evolving. Each time, using a set interval of time, one must be satisfied with what one is able to understand, perhaps linking it to previous knowledge.[2] In addition to the Southern experience, what fol-

---

[2] One way to intuitively test this idea is to retrace our steps for a moment. The "intriguing" aspect of the relationship between Italy and the United States lies precisely in the importance of the convergences, divergences and even oppositions that connect them (Meldolesi 1985). Young Italians landing in the United States find a culture different from their own that is nevertheless very useful. On the other hand, Americans who fall in love with Italian culture appreciate its diversity and try (in their own way) to take possession of it. In the inevitable oscillation of such feelings, it is interesting to note that in 1998-99, also thanks to Benigni and Bocelli (two Tuscans par excellence), the US recorded an important pro-Italian resurgence.

lows stems also from an interest in a number of Eastern countries, several trips to Berlin, the former GDR, and also a specific opportunity — a Harvard-MIT conference on political strategies for economic development in East Germany and Southern Italy, where I was assigned the role of "revisiting" the Mezzogiorno (March 1998).

The Mezzogiorno Revisited

The emphasis of the conference was (inevitably) on the ongoing process of change in the two areas. After the fall of the Berlin Wall, the entire center of gravity of European construction began to shift eastward, much to the dismay of the French. It is a development that seems to follow the long stride of history — of an entire epoch that from the eighteenth-century cultural renaissance of "*Mitteleuropa*," and surviving the conflicts of the nineteenth century followed by two "hot" wars and one "cold," seems finally to be unveiling a horizon of peace and prosperity for the entire area.

The single currency itself, which binds the various participants in the general functioning of the European Union, seems to fit with this development — supposing that the process of transition from socialism to the democratic market-economy system can gradually be mastered (which is by no means easy).

And what about the Mezzogiorno? Should it not also be discussed as part of the area in which it is located? Shouldn't it benefit, in the medium term, from the unfreezing of energy produced by the democratic revolution of 1989-91? These are awkward questions because they do not reflect the way we look at things. Locked in a sort of self-referential provincialism, we cling to the hardly creative[3] idea that our area is a special

---

[3] Indeed, it is reminiscent of the "tropical" claim of some Colombian intellectuals of the 1950s, who asserted with some malice (Hirschman 1986, p. 8), "Aqui en el tropico hacemos todo al revés" [Here in the tropics we do everything backwards].

46

case. We used to think that the Italian Communist Party had little to do with Moscow; now we tend to believe that the institutional, political and economic troubles we find ourselves in are strictly "homegrown."

This is not so. If the Cold War long divided German territory, it split Italian society as well. If the ex-communist public system of Eastern Europe "weeps," the Italian one "is not amused." If the ashes of real socialism leave behind a trail of recriminations, our country must bid farewell to an entire era and find the pace of this greater cohesion.

Seeing things from this point of view, the comparison between East Germany and the Mezzogiorno takes on the sense of a bold comparison between two very different areas that nevertheless both fall into the EU's "Objective I" (structural funds), and have a serious official unemployment problem. In addition, both suffered severely from the Cold War, during which the one was violently transformed into a kind of tragic showcase for "socialism," while the other was sacrificed on the altar of Western *realpolitik* — a necessity that, as the South was bent to support centralized power, required closing both eyes to the worsening of the area's well-known pathologies.

The method mentioned requires us to collect our thoughts regarding both these contexts. And since my role in the Cambridge (MA) conference was to present the Mezzogiorno, I will first reprise the notes I prepared for that occasion.

My line of thinking originated from a 1996 pamphlet by a well-known Italian diplomat, Ludovico Incisa di Camerana, *Italy Won the Third World War* — that is, the Cold War.[4] This is

---

They were instinctively protecting their own distinctiveness, while at the same time — as I understand it — precluding themselves from the possibility of fully affirming their own ideas. My intent, of course, is to give the game away — that is, to identify the areas of general convergence in order to give due weight to those that are indigenous and creative.

[4] Just as the second post-World War period was marked by the Republican

historically true. But it is also true that our country did not want to admit it. Had it done so, it would have had to come to grips with a tangled mess.

Historical judgment (obviously) vindicates the political forces that won—those in the West, pro-government during the First Republic. But it was these same forces that then decomposed as an indirect consequence of that victory. To recognize that Italy won World War III while it lost World War II and thus, like Germany, could emerge from the unnatural condition in which it was constricted is to point to the particular "contortions" that exist in the background of Italian political life. During the Cold War, the opposition had no outlet and, despite its merits, often ended up in a cul-de-sac. Today, on the other hand, after various reversals, those who were on the "wrong side" are the main force in the governmental majority. How can it presume to win the peace at the end of a war it lost? And, yet, this is the problem.

It is not enough, clearly, to change the names and programs of the political leaders. It is necessary to bring about a progressive and profound mental change in voters and political and trade union militants. Through a process that is certainly not yet concluded the ex-communist democratic left, in concert with its allies, has to learn how best to manage our Western society, and has to seize the opportunities generated by the international realignment. In other words, it has to know how to dissolve and regenerate itself in the much broader democratic environment that is in the process of being recomposed.

Maybe haphazardly, piecemeal, or clumsily (as in the case of illegal immigration and the Kosovo war) the hundred Souths

---

Constitution, the Atlantic choice and reconstruction, so the third—following the Cold War—could be characterized by the European choice, the gradual rise of the Mezzogiorno and the need to redesign the economic-normative functioning of Italian society in general.

are regaining awareness of their geo-economic location and the opportunities it offers. The South-North "bottleneck" — or rather the one between one's own neighborhood and the media-driven North that towers over everything — is shrinking. Even EU Mediterranean policy, long the Cinderella story in Southern minds, is starting to be looked at in a different way. Everywhere there is an incipient need to come out of the shell.

The civic recovery of the 1990s, after producing a certain cultural, institutional and productive reorientation, is turning into self-rediscovery, a rediscovery of the South's own regional societies, and their inter-linkages and potentials. The emphasis that is often placed on the "communal revolution" of 1993 (see, for example, Sales 1999 and Macry 1999) hints at the reality of this broader process, which has yet to see its fruit effectively ripen at the local and regional levels.

If one goes back in memory to the "conniving" of the dominant forces of the First Republic and the entrenched culture of an opposition that was discriminated against, it must be acknowledged that the step was great. But if we then ask ourselves what should be done, then we are forced to recognize that between clientelist-corporatist populism, the technical-aristocratic mentality, and how we would need to behave to take proper advantage of today's opportunities, there is unfortunately a wide field to cross, full of inertia and pitfalls.

This clarifies the "spirit of the times." Engrossed as we are by daily difficulties, we fail to situate our work within a medium-term project. Conversely, when we set aside everyday concerns, as we have up to now, to focus on the frame of reference, we know full well that a pedestrian *redde rationem* awaits us at the end of the road. What would be the point of scanning the horizon if we could not translate the lessons learned into concrete facts?

It is a problem that has similar characteristics on both sides of the former Iron Curtain. It involves holding tight to the interactions that fortunately bind together the different times in the history of our countries — the certainties of the past, the convulsive present and the hypothetical future.[5]

A Look at the Facts

The populist high tide of the last phase of the Cold War, as I argued in my Cambridge notes, pushed public spending, as a percentage of income in the South — this is an official figure — to the astronomical level of 73 percent (1989; two-thirds of which was composed of public salaries and transfers). This percentage then gradually declined and with it the net flow of resources to the South. After the 1992 slump, net imports of goods and services as a percentage of available resources fell from 15.5 to 11.7 (1997).[6] Public debt repayment produced a major redistribution to the detriment of the South. This forced the Southern economy into a dangerous slump that primarily affected agriculture, construction, trade and the banking system.[7]

Between 1992 and 1997, output in the South grew by 1.8 percent (compared with 8.5 in the North-Center).[8] Investment

---

[5] This point is in a sense the mirror image of the one raised by Hirschman in his critique at the Annales school (1986, ch. 8). While he claims possibilist discretion with respect to historical trend, I am seeking here to do the reverse — that is, to use positive historical trends, near and far, to ward off the looming danger of short-term disorientation. As will become clear later, I think both viewpoints are useful. Indeed, they should be fully developed on their merits without losing sight of each other.

[6] In the 1980s such transfers averaged 17%, while at the beginning of the decade they had been at 19%.

[7] As is well known, the southern credit system had to bring out hidden non-performing loans, go through an accelerated restructuring process and often ended up in the hands of others. (To offer an idea: in 1995 the Bank of Naples lost more than 3,000 billion, Sicilcassa more than 1,000, ISVEIMER 600, the Bank of Sicily 274, etc.). In addition, the South experienced substantial growth in labor costs as a result of phasing out social security relief.

[8] Combined with a higher population growth rate than the European average, this trend has reopened the gap between the per capita income of the Mezzogiorno and the average income of the Union. In particular, when comparing the 1988-90

in public works fell by more than half. The number of declared jobs declined by six hundred thousand, while the official unemployment rate jumped above 20 percent (and then rose again to nearly 23 percent—1996).

Fortunately, this is not the whole story. As the change of regime in East Germany was called the "Wende" (turning point) so too for the South there is talk of a turning point[9]—even though a better way of putting it would be "first steps." The abolition of Intervento Straordinario, the decrease in public spending and the influx of resources from outside reduced "welfarism" and in part nudged industry toward the market and exports—which grew significantly despite starting from a modest level. In addition, the reorientation of businesses altered the Southern landscape, as formerly backward areas forged ahead while others lost ground. (For example: data from the Intermediate Industrial Census, 1996, produced with a new methodology, call attention to products "made in Italy" from Abruzzo, Puglia and Campania—but those familiar with the area know that there is also a flurry of initiatives elsewhere, sometimes intermittent.)[10]

Far be it from me—as I argued in the Cambridge discussion—to question the moderate optimism (or perhaps one might say the anxious anticipation) that arises from this. Rather, as a professor of economic policy and as an advisor to the

---

and 1994-96 averages, the largest regions—Campania, Puglia and Sicily—suffered a relative deterioration. And as for investments, between 1992 and 1997 there was an estimated cumulative contraction of almost 24 percent (30 percent in construction, 15.7 in investment in machinery, equipment and means of transport, which, however, in 1996-97 appeared to be recovering slightly).

[9] For example, in Bodo and Viesti (1997).

[10] Finally, a certain improvement in municipal administration, a greater European presence, a tendency toward social awakening and a new impetus toward productive enterprise completed a picture that subsequently continued to brighten in terms of the birth-mortality of VAT accounts, exports and even (embryonically) of employment.

government, I have long argued for the need to intensify efforts to understand and take action to achieve better outcomes. To return to Incisa di Camerana, it is true that in recent times Italy has become more confident that it can win the peace after winning the war and that the Mezzogiorno has become a test case for such a policy. But this is certainly not an easy task because it means further reducing welfarism, freeing up energy that can be employed productively, regularizing the Mezzogiorno in stages, increasing regular employment, making the administration work, and so on. Not only that—we need to support market access in the South and focus efforts on unleashing its internal potential, including that of production systems with a local focus.

It is important, however, that this new situation has at least presented itself and that even in official circles the eventual rise of the Mezzogiorno is now considered within the realm of possibility.

Ten years ago, at the height of the welfare crisis in the South (Meldolesi 1990), I argued for the need for a liberal and progressive policy that would push Southern producers to engage with the market (in such a way as to change their behavior and, through cognitive dissonance, their motivations as well) and would at the same time support them in coping with competition. I see with pleasure that a somewhat similar line of reasoning now opens an insert of *Il Mulino* on "The Development of the South." "Who more than the Mezzogiorno," writes Paolo Macry in *L'occasione meridionale*, [The Southern Opportunity], 1999, p. 812, "would stand to gain from decentralization, deregulation, the liberalization of the market, the downsizing of monopolies, the affirmation of a culture of merit, in short, from the end of privileges and rigged games?" My logical requirement of ten years ago thus takes on the appearance of a historically possible event. Relieved of the weight that the interests of the old economic and political system still exert in other areas of the country, as Macry adds, the South, or rather the South that manages to free itself from clientelist and corporate loyalties, could prove to be ready for the process of modernization much sooner than expected.

Behavior and Policy

Let us take a step back to clarify the issue. In opening his last book of essays—*Scritti sul Mezzogiorno* [Writings on the Mezzogiorno] (1982)—Manlio Rossi-Doria wrote that "the Southern reality had been rapidly evolving, and even more rapidly, the policies in which I had been a participant—even if a critical supporter [...]—had become worn out and exhausted. The discussion about changes in the Southern situation and revising the policies affecting it is now more open than ever. It will be the young people who will take it up and carry it forward."

But a new point of view was struggling to emerge. In the 1980s, traditional approaches continued to dominate the scene, while corresponding policies increasingly took a welfarist turn. Southerners in the vast majority understood themselves through an intellectual archetype analogous to what Hirschman (1971, 1995) called "a pessimistic outlook that urges action" ("If you want to get along, complain" says a caustic Sicilian proverb). Thus, cause and effect in the overall degradation of the political-institutional system increased the discrepancy between reality and the growing demand for public money. At a certain point someone began to read the traditional paradigm in reverse—instead of wishing for additional public funding to compensate for a situation that tended to worsen, the question was why increased spending was correlated with negative results.

Thus, at the turn of the 1980s-1990s there was a process of rethinking aimed at breaking free from the traditional way of thinking. We were seeking a new understanding of the Mezzogiorno, an alternative point of view, honest enough to confront the incredible current degradation of social and political life (Pezzino 1992, Trigilia 1992, Meldolesi 1992a). In the end, an idea largely underestimated by traditional Meridionalism began to make headway—in economic growth, behavior matters. And how!

In the postwar period, development economists generally assumed that actors behaved like the so-called "homo oeconomicus." Italian sociologists, on the other hand, opposed the amoral familism thesis that Edward Banfield had proposed in 1958 in his study of Chiaromonte (Montegrano). In so doing they inadvertently blocked research on this decisive issue. Only Ignazio Silone (1968) anticipated with great lucidity what we were to theorize a quarter of a century later.

Amoral familism, lack of civicness and social capital (Putnam 1993) or "maladie d'amour" (Meldolesi 1992a) are different ways of describing individual and collective behaviors in the Mezzogiorno that do not lead to socio-economic development. The welfarist high tide of the 1980s represented the acme of the social degradation brought on by the interaction of a disturbing mass pathological trend with the political-institutional system of the time.

The emergency was dealt with, but the problem remains. Development in the South cannot be discussed in the current language of more market or more state intervention. The focus should instead be on welfarism versus policies that oppose corporatism and free-riding and are anti-clientelist and even anti-criminal. Once this line of demarcation has been drawn, the aim must then be a reasonable mix of market and state for development policies. This is precisely a "liberal and progressive" solution of a better market (more free, more integrated into the European system) and a better state (more effective and efficient, more growth-oriented) (Meldolesi 1992a, 1998a). With this we can return to Macry's reasoning. Suppose, as he argues, that the South may be edging closer to "late comer" behavior (because of the lack on the ground of heavy-handed social and political organizations that tend to perpetuate the structural and regulatory framework in which they have established themselves, because of the sharp reduction in public transfers and state-owned enterprises mentioned above, because of the very modest participation of the South in national welfare, because of the South's anti-bureaucratic and anti-centralist politicking, because of the somewhat surprising revival of its public spirit, because of a growing thicket of tangible structural signs, etc.). Is it enough to affirm with Macry (1999, p. 811) that "what this South is asking of the government is rules (or new rules) against the bureaucratic swamp, freedom of work and enterprise, an end to the tangle of large and small extortions (material and moral) that are typical of statist economies, reclamation of the territory from racketeering [...] reform of local powers and fiscal federalism"?

Or is it instead the case that in the interaction, not always consistent, between a Mezzogiorno seeking its own evolutionary path and a government that must reconcile the pace of modernization with political equilibrium, we should take Albert Hirschman's view of the late-late comer (as opposed to Alexander Gerschenkron's classic view: cf. Gerschenkron 1961; Hirschman 1971, ch. 3, 1986, p. 26; Meldolesi 1995, pp. 79-87), recognizing the need to divide the path into viable segments and to take action to ensure that they are actually traveled?

In other words, sensing "a window of opportunity" does not mean seizing it. The focus — in my opinion — must be on the knots that need loosening and on how to strengthen the ongoing process by empowering the territorial setting and by involving and gradually redirecting growing parts of the administrative, local and central political system.

Lights and shadows

Fortunately, in everyday life, pathological behavior is mixed with behavior that is anything but. Even during the populist high tide, traditional peasant values prevailed in significant parts of the South—work, thrift and saving. Moreover, in the South—no use denying it—it is "wrong thinking," that often prevails—the temptation of deviousness, etc. So that beyond the family and relationships between relatives and friends "trust and mutual respect" (Adizes 1988) are scarce. But they are not absent. It is a scarcity that sometimes arises from fear and suffering which can partly be remedied by a process of internal recovery. On the other hand, if the Southern economy were able to expand vigorously and in an orderly and sustained way, if it adequately rewarded positive behavior (and robustly discouraged negative), confidence could grow.

As mentioned above, the Mezzogiorno has already witnessed the beginnings of light industrialization based on small businesses (which has partly taken up preexisting artisan vocations, weakened but not dissolved by the post-war situation: see Meldolesi, Aniello, eds., 1998). A portion of these SMEs captured some measure of public funding—but the vast majority went it alone. Southern small businesses—white, black and especially "caffè e latte" ["coffee with milk"][11]—work for the con-

---

[11] This expression came to me spontaneously on the sidelines of the conference. The vogue of subdividing the Italian habit of mixing milk with coffee into a hundred mini-recipes had exploded in the United States—from *latte macchiato* to black coffee and passing, of course, through *cappuccino*. It was this amusing surprise that suggested to me, by association, the idea of the coffee and milk economy. By this I mean that if it is true, as CENSIS claims, that almost half of Italian businesses do not operate on a completely legal basis, this percentage

tract market. They often represent the other side of the sometimes somewhat hagiographic story of the Italian districts and local systems. The industrial districts of the Center-North and the associated Southern producers scattered across the territory are like a workshop with its backrooms. This arrangement has long been ignored, but today its raised voices are demanding emancipation and improved access to the European and international markets and have achieved some important results.

In the early 1990s, anti-Meridionalist sentiment in the North — some of it (paradoxically) from former emigrants from the South dissatisfied with their situation after so much work — was exploited by the Northern League to glorify Padania and later secessionism. It has therefore become important to show that things in the South are not as depressing as they were being depicted.

If nothing else, many Southerners get up early in the morning and go to work in the fields, workshops and small businesses. Many of the so-called "Made in Italy" household and personal products, although manufactured in the South, reach the end market via the Center-North — people in Italy or abroad who buy a wallet from Florence or glass from Murano certainly don't ask about such things.

Moreover, the number of micro-enterprises and their growth rate are astonishing in a number of areas. Is it not possible that, by vigorously supporting the productive efforts of these small businesses, we might end up changing the "balance of behavior" (between fresh entrepreneurship on the one hand and the mentality of the fixed job and the gentry on the other) and with it the social-political condition of so many areas?

This eventuality, together with the semi-submerged nature

---

clearly increases in the South. Milk-white enterprises in the Mezzogiorno are in a clear minority, while the large army of small and very small enterprises add varying doses of coffee.

of much of Southern light industry lent an unexpected quality to our field research — it won over scores of young researchers and intrigued the press. A step was taken in redressing the Southern balance — only a step. The different aspects of the Hirschmanian development strategy — analysis, policies, programs, exit routes, applications, monitoring, evaluation, reorientation — have not yet found a coherent solution. To sketch one out, a number of (positive) strands must be brought into the initiative and others neutralized or fought against. For example — the Mezzogiorno is still, for the most part, a disorganized society. Few follow the letter, much less the spirit of the law. The amount of illegality among individuals, households, businesses and the administration vary enormously in level and percentage. A reasonable policy ought to focus on the suppression of crimes serious enough to incur certain punishment and should at the same time stimulate a vigorous process of gradual regularization, little by little (directly and indirectly) imposing higher civil standards within a framework of development and collective emancipation.

Unfortunately, parasitism and cronyism often turn out to be legal or legalized, while the underground economy (even the burgeoning economy of young people involved in high tech) is by its very nature irregular. It is a contrast that speaks volumes about the social injustice that still exists in the Mezzogiorno. The balance of power between income and labor (self-employed and subordinate) and between the non-productive and productive parts of society often favors the former. This clearly poses a very delicate problem. The growth of the economic and social clout of small businesses would in many situations undoubtedly alter those traditional relationships that are still the preserve of professional "mediators": magistrates, notaries, lawyers, teachers, etc. But it would require regularization and thus a strengthening of small businesses so as to absorb the cost.

Again, in a region with such a large part of the economy underground, it is inevitable that young people will be looking for jobs that are better and more regular than those available. It thus happens that much of Southern unemployment sits on top of the underground economy and often also on top of the regular work of small businesses — while non-EU immigration occupies the jobs at the base of the pyramid and in some areas forms of poverty and social decay emerge. The problem of motivating young people and actively engaging them in the development of the production system takes center stage.

But in the process of recalling these different aspects of the "Southern condition" we are drawn into (indeed entangled in) their complexity, with the danger — as mentioned — of once again losing our overall orientation.

Regaining some distance from everyday life may therefore prove to be a useful exercise for at least two reasons. First: if we trace back to the Mezzogiorno the "management difficulties" we diagnosed for the country as a whole, we find that they take on an ambivalent connotation. The greater social distance of the Southern aristocratic tradition leads to a worsening of the problem. On the other hand, it is also true that precisely because of this it is easier to break free of it, to think about change based on free enterprise. (This, undoubtedly, is the attraction of the United States for so many young Southerners).

On the other hand, as mentioned above, change must permeate and implicate the public system. It is a *changement de coeur* that may seem impossible but is perhaps not as far off as we might think. To be convinced of this, it is useful to read the "historiographical revisionism" concerning the formation of the nineteenth-century Southern ruling classes and their half-hearted insertion into the unified state (Pezzino 1999)[12]. It is worth reflecting on how this problem passed through Fascism and the post-World War II period, to arrive finally at a question that has surfaced recently as an unintentional effect of the Northern League polemic. How can we act so that gradually all institutions — from municipal to regional to central — are felt by Southern Italians to actually be theirs?

An Upside-down Comparison

All right, the reader will think, but what does this have to do with East Germany? Shouldn't the Mezzogiorno be compared to other regions of southern Europe or, perhaps, to parts of Mexico that gravitate toward the United States?

Certainly, such comparisons would not be off base (see Appendix). But it is not necessarily the case that a comparison of similar situations is best for getting us into the comparative problem. Moreover, we are not precluded from learning something unexpected from other sources. Another reason is that I would like to test experimentally the methodological propensity mentioned above — the socio-anthropologically inspired inclination to compare aspects that are near and far. In fact — in my opinion — the appeal of the comparison between Southern Italy and East Germany does not lie in the convergence between the two areas as such — that is, in the thesis dear to some

---

[12] "In the South," wrote Paolo Pezzino (1999, pp. 63-4), "there were [...] few structures, (associative or institutional) that supported and channeled social consensus toward a basic loyalty to the system [...]. Nevertheless, in these regions [...] a precociousness of political experience [...] produced perverse effects — local elites rushed to occupy the new spaces opened up by the political system without really sharing its ultimate aims. This provoked a permanent distrust on the part of institutions towards this civil society, its rules, its customs [abundantly documented by the reports of administrators before the Unification, and of prefects and magistrates immediately after], which was not matched by an ability to establish legitimizing institutional practices."

German intellectuals that the former GDR is the German Mezzogiorno. Rather, as bizarre as it seems, such a comparison allows us to focus on distinctive features of two contexts, even very different ones, that we would not otherwise have observed in such a light.

At first glance the comparison between East Germany and the South appears "impossible," especially if it is drawn in very general terms. While East Germany is home to regions prominent in German history (such as Saxony, Thuringia, and parts of Prussia), the Mezzogiorno, despite its objective weight, played a central role in the Italian economy only in ancient times. While East Germany has long had a significant industrial base, the economic structure of Mezzogiorno was predominantly agricultural right up to the postwar period. While in the former GDR, public intervention following reunification quickly achieved considerable results (in terms of aggregate product, investment, and infrastructure), the Intervento Straordinario targeting the Mezzogiorno, after a promising first phase, experienced a long decline (and an inglorious epilogue). While Berlin as capital and the eastward enlargement of the European Union prefigure a new leading role for the *Neue Bundesländer*, the same cannot be said for the Italian South.

But looking at things more closely — that is, looking at the current functioning of the two areas — the comparison becomes more compelling.

We can start with a visual image. Berlin and Rome are now two capitals that have become largely detached from the "industrial heartland" of their respective countries. They have lost the leading international political function they had during the Cold War and, despite their efforts to reactivate their role in a new way, they understand their medium-term prospects are tied to the development of the "lagging" areas — the former GDR and the Mezzogiorno — that gravitate to them. This is even more true for the development of the vast world surrounding them to the east and south and to the southeast, respectively.

On the "fate" of the GDR (i.e., how and why an unexpected internal convulsion buried it as a political entity) Albert Hirschman wrote enlightening pages (1995, ch. 1). Thereafter, as is well known, East-German firms were not equal to the competition. The revaluation of the East Mark by more than 300 percent as dictated by the political emergency — that is, by the need to exploit the Gorbachevian momentum and create an immediate consensus for reunification[13] — and the transformation of reunification into a kind of annexation[14] dealt a death blow to the East German economy.

Production fell to one-third of what it had been, and employment collapsed. In a couple of years, a region that was on paper hyper-industrialized suddenly became de-industrialized.[15] The hundreds of public programs for infrastructure, labor, welfare, local government and development, and the great

[13] To keep the new fellow citizens at home and prevent them from "voting with their feet" by moving to the West, Chancellor Kohl thought they should be guaranteed an income like that of the average West German. Hence the decision to immediately liberalize the movement of people and things, to exchange the mark at parity, and to undertake a vast aid program (financed mostly by an increase in German public debt, which in fact doubled).

[14] It all happened within a few months after the elections in the GDR on March 18, 1990, won by the CDU. On July 1, the Treaty on German Economic Monetary and Social Union came into force. But the decline of the economy of the eastern Länder continued, as did mass emigration to West Germany. Bonn then decided to move quickly toward political union and implemented Article 23 of the 1949 "Provisional" Constitution of the Federal Republic, known as the "Basic Law." "The choice of Article 23 corresponded to the fundamental decision to rebuild East Germany in the image of West Germany and represented the rejection of Article 146, which advocated the dissolution of the Basic Law and the writing of a new constitution for all Germans. The unification treaty negotiated by representatives of the Federal Republic and the Democratic Republic was signed on August 31, 1990" (Locke, Trigilia, p. 7). West German laws and institutions were quickly transferred to the East. Government agencies, banks, trade unions, business associations and West-German welfare programs were quickly installed in the former GDR.

[15] With the partial exception of Saxony, recovered through a program designed and executed by administrative and industrial personnel imported from the West.

program of privatization and business restructuring, despite their effective generosity, failed to effectively alleviate the situation.[16] The new productive apparatus, born out of privatization, was poorly rooted in society and often dependent on the outside.[17]

In many areas the intervention failed to stimulate the local entrepreneurship and economic dynamism that would have been needed—on the contrary, the impression was that it was stifling it. This process, argued Richard Locke and Carlo Trigilia (1998), was the opposite of what occurred in the Mezzogiorno, where the reduction of welfare-type public intervention fostered productive redirection and the emergence of a certain entrepreneurial vitality at the local level.[18] The relations between the two regions—they argue with an appealing formula—are "mirror images."

Perhaps this is not entirely the case. But instead of arguing this point, it is first worth exploring the reasoning of the two authors. First, at the time of unification much of the DDR's industrial production, the pride of socialism, suddenly lost its internal and external (socialist) markets. Intervention allowed a substitution of income—unit wages, private consumption and

---

[16] The financial transfer from West Germany to East Germany was massive. Overall, it hovered around 5 percent of the former's income and 40 percent of the latter's per year. According to some estimates, the subsidies obtained in various capacities affected 30 percent of the labor force.

[17] Numerous facilities reported to leadership found elsewhere. The average size of businesses was smaller than in West Germany. The regional economic network was so much weaker that even in Saxony, the main industrial center of the GDR, 75 percent of firms ordered the vast majority of their supplies from outside the region.

[18] "Up to a certain point," the two authors write, (p. 4), "the experience of the Italian South represents the reverse image (of that of East Germany). Looking at the aggregate data, the economic situation in the Mezzogiorno clearly deteriorated during the 1990s. However, at the micro level one can identify interesting cases of local dynamism and clusters of small and medium-sized enterprises strongly rooted in their local society." Locke and Trigilia's text reconstructs the story of the Mezzogiorno since the postwar period. But my impression is that the comparison makes more sense if we limit it to more recent years and develop it in detail.

total income in East Germany grew, while employment plummeted. It was nearly 10 million in the DDR, declined to just 5.5 million in 1995 and then slowly recovered in subsequent years. The official unemployment rate is 15 percent.

Moreover, a possibly equivalent amount of unemployment is masked by labor policies (training, retraining, part-time, early retirement, etc.). According to some observers, about half of the transfers take the form of subsidies. Moreover, the part allocated to investment is linked to the boom in construction and local consumption demand — it essentially depends on the continuation of the intervention. The high rate of new business creation has unfortunately been accompanied by a high rate of bankruptcies, while East German exports are only 2 percent of all German exports (Locke, Trigilia 1998, pp. 80 and 31-3).

Arguably, the difficulties of "adjustment" are magnified by a population that would like the advantages of the market economy without actually adjusting to the new conditions. But the structural condition just described exists and can be seen. Traveling off the beaten path in East Germany, it is immediately clear that the transformation has pushed a large section of the population to the margins, a lower tier that has fallen into a condition of assisted and resentful semi-passivity. The collapse of employment suddenly loosened the labor market. Coming from a safe job, many workers were faced with a weak market they were not at all prepared for.[19] "The reaction of the people of the eastern Länder," writes Marcello de Cecco in his Berlin Diary (1999), "is the best proof that in our society the only social legitimacy is provided by work."[20]

---

[19] Later, however, a study commissioned by the government collected significant data on a broader industrial recovery (German Brief 1998).

[20] "The East Germans," de Cecco continues, "were not at all amused by this experiment that turned them into pure consumers. Not least because many positions of some importance and responsibility, on their own territory, were taken from them and unceremoniously handed over to West Germans. Not only in industry, but also,

Reasons for an "inspiration"

Locke and Trigilia's reasoning has opened a door in the work of comparing the Mezzogiorno and East Germany. My impression is that it needs to develop further by delving into the specifics of their respective contexts. What led me to this idea were the papers by Ingrid Artus (1998) and Katharina Bluhm (1998) of the University of Jena presented at the Cambridge (MA) Conference and devoted respectively to industrial relations and business cooperation in the former GDR.

Indeed, I learned from Artus's essay that in order to compete, many East German firms seek to deviate in part from national labor contracts by not joining trade associations, negotiating special clauses with unions, and agreeing informally with workers. I also learned that somewhat different forms of industrial relations have developed in East Germany, less institutionalized and less corporate forms, which Artus calls "cohesive enterprise communities with a rigid nature," "cooperative forms oriented toward integration and co-management," and "authoritarian regimes dominated by management." I learned further that in East Germany undeclared work as a first job is widespread in some sectors (especially in construction) but does not play a major role. Finally, I thought that the issue of inter-firm cooperation studied by Bluhm (who hotly disputes some oversimplified generalizations about the East German situation and intelligently examines the evolution of enterprises in the region and the formation of local systems) might unfold more thoroughly if it used the Mezzogiorno's district-oriented local systems as a counterpoint.

On the other hand, there is no doubt in my mind that from a Southern point of view the recent history of Germany is instructive, a key opening the mind.

---

and especially, in the civil service and teaching, especially in universities."

Living for a long time on the opposite side of the Iron Curtain, the Mezzogiorno and East Länder went through different experiences. With the fall of the Berlin Wall, both suffered trauma. For a variety of reasons, the East German episode took on a particularly dramatic character. The long-awaited unification turned into a clash between "Wessis" (Westerners) and "Ossis" (Easterners). Contradicting the historically typical German tendency toward social acquiescence, the latter — the Saxons and Prussians — found the courage to free themselves from dictatorship, but for reasons of expediency and revenge they were ripped by the "Wessis" as good-for-nothings and often perceived events as a humiliation. Hence a rather troubling psychological gulf has emerged.[21]

Moreover, despite the best efforts, unification brought out the economic gap that had formed over time between the Federal Republic and the GDR. Along with the psychological antagonism the structural asymmetries between the two parts of Germany came to the fore — serious problems that we know well in the South and that need to be dealt with intelligently.

In the East, the network of enterprises is less solid, they are smaller and more hetero directed than those in West Germany. They tend to have a more modest bargaining position, in a social setting still characterized by strong resentment, mass unemployment, welfare, early retirement, youth distress, etc.

Deja vu of the Mezzogiorno? That is to say: a direct relationship? It is not. And neither is the inverse relationship ad-

---

[21] "The Ossis," de Cecco writes again, "got money, lots of money, but only provided they would get out of the way and let their saviors work to rebuild their country, which — as they were reminded every day — they had allowed to degrade to levels unworthy of German pride. So, since Germany is a democratic country, the only means of expressing themselves they were left with was voting against both the government and the opposition — that is for the revived Communist Party and for the menacing neo-Nazi groups springing up like mushrooms in the East."

vocated by Locke and Trigilia. Rather, they are direct and inverse aspects[22] of a single very complex and intriguing relationship.

Probably, interest generated by comparing the two situations is based on affinities and dissimilarities, even at a distance, between different characteristics. Indeed, going into the specifics of their respective experiences, the two societies manage to talk to each other, perhaps by analogy — in the sense that knowledge of certain aspects of one spontaneously raises questions of various kinds about those of the other, helping to bring them into focus, to interpret them. It is the initially unlikely (but possible) quality of the multifaceted relationship between such areas that surprisingly ignites our imagination and enables us to observe reality in a new way.[23]

First takeaway — the key question that must be asked is not, as currently maintained, whether two social settings are comparable, but whether their comparison is more or less fruitful, and why. In this regard, one should be wary of simplified formulas and putting things in "boxes." Similarity and difference, repetition and uniqueness are intermingled "in nature" and re-

---

[22] Inverse aspects of the relationship are not as rare as it might seem. Alongside that of Locke and Trigilia, for example, one can cite Albert Hirschman's example (1995, ch. 17) of the industrialization of Eastern European countries and Latin America, which undoubtedly also applies to East Germany and Mezzogiorno. In fact, these large Objective 1 areas of the EU are unhappy with the lack of industrialization but also with the type of industrialization—East Germany because it had industrialization based on core industry, Mezzogiorno (until the day before yesterday) because it did not have core industry. Probably Southerners' own underestimation of Southern Made in Italy also has this origin.

[23] The reader of things Colornian-Hirschmanian will have come to grips with what I have in mind. The comparison makes sense because it allows us to highlight and thus learn things we did not know. These are things that surprise us — we did not expect to encounter them because we had not looked at them from the vantage point of that comparison, with its many components and types of relationship. They are improbable *ex-ante* acquisitions that instead prove possible and by this route mentally lead us into an unexpected cognitive-normative field.

sult in ever new solutions. It thus happens that some experiences speak to each other, some not so much, some not at all. It depends on their conformation—on what they have in common, what is different, reversed, neutral, or unclassifiable about each of them and how they combine. Something in this constellation helps us think, encourages us, suggests that we reason in a different way. Sometimes it is difficult to say *exactly* where such "inspiration" comes from, as when we think we have identified a specific correlation that instead, on further examination, gets out of hand, or when a phenomenon that is initially insignificant turns out later to be full of leads. What is certain is that it is worthwhile to educate our capacities of comparison so that they increase the cognitive spectrum on existing potentials and thus increase the freedom we have and the choices (individual and collective) available to us.

Second takeaway: An earlier version of this essay, "launched" like a little boat among my Neapolitan students during the 1998-99 academic year aroused much interest. Perhaps it was because—it occurred to me—Southerners feel even more boxed in by the South-Germany relationship than the South-North one—have you ever happened to meet an emigrant on some train extolling the merits of German discipline?

It happened, then, that my students felt attracted (and ennobled) by an unexpected comparison. Its "peculiar" nature, which they said they would never have thought of, set their capacity for comparison in motion. From here a more general consequence can be drawn "in reverse." Attracted by the Northern way of life, but diminished and inert in the face of media hammering, too many Southerners tend to passively reproduce in their little corner Northern styles of consumption, without being able to react, compare, or understand. Hence, it becomes important to find useful stratagems to foster a different kind of awareness.

I confess that the reaction of my students was not entirely unexpected. From the beginning of the conference at MIT, the comparison between the Italian South and the German East had not only seemed useful in itself, it had seemed expedient (ingenious, advantageous) as a tool—as bait, if you like—to accustom the mind to confrontation, a need especially felt at a time when Southern culture (from historical to economic) is showing some signs of revival. In other words, the passion to question why a person is the way they are and what they should do has been reborn in the South. But this has not yet produced a real interest in opening fruitful relations in an upward direction, or in exchanging experiences and suggestions among the different Mezzogiornos, or even in situating the Mezzogiorno in the geosocial environment in which it finds itself—all activities which, as we shall now see, require the development of comparative analysis.

To activate our comparative sense, it is often worth unearthing an unexpected margin of empathy. My students felt close to East Germans because they recognized certain structural features they knew about, but also because they learned about extraordinary events, they were largely unaware of that made other European citizens feel more "human" to them.

It is not necessarily just a matter of solidarity between people who have been discriminated against. It is possible for the empathy mechanism to be set in motion on the positive side — encountering in detail the reasons for another's success may bring home a useful lesson to ourselves. In short, things begin to move into gear when observing others encourages us to reexamine or even discover certain characteristics of our own, perhaps by opposition, association of ideas, etc. This is advisable work in any case, because it helps trigger the learning mechanism that in every age has mad "catching up" easier for lagging countries.

On the other hand, the condition of asymmetry spontaneously accentuates high-low relations at the expense of horizontal ones, especially those that are inter-regional. How many telephone, e-mail, epistolary exchanges are there between Taranto and Cosenza? How many Palermitans know what is happening in Cagliari or Salerno? If a comparative mindset is developed these vast gray areas of our understanding of the South can gradually shrink.[24]

Finally, the Mezzogiorno, the different Mezzogiornos urgently need to initiate a comparative analysis with the countries around them. Along with reducing cultural distances, they need to set aside the sense of superiority that separates them from Africa and the Balkans. Those who, like me, were in Sicily as a boy and experienced firsthand the extraordinary revolution in customs that has occurred on the island (and in the entire South), cannot help but hope that by circuitous routes this whiff of emancipation — especially for women — will finally cross the channel that separates us from Africa's North. But to track the evolution of this hypothesis one would need to know, in terms of information, empathy, and comparison, what is happening throughout *mare nostrum* – the Arab shore included.

APPENDIX

Intra-Southern comparisons

This is a point worth pressing. Southerners often talk about the South, but they actually mean their own home. It is not easy

---

[24] This is more difficult than it would seem because it requires abandoning inveterate habits and coming into contact with multiple worlds — perhaps varying them and becoming passionate about one or the other so as to gradually ignite one's comparative understanding. Of course, it could be argued, if a daring comparison such as that between Southern Italy and East Germany is possible, why should we find it difficult to study Lecce and Siracusa? Actually, the reverse is true — that is to say, in order to convince ourselves of the usefulness of such home-grown comparisons, it is somewhat bizarre (but instructive) that we had to do so by way of Leipzig and Jena.

to meet a Sicilian who is passionate about things Neapolitan or a Campanian about events in Puglia. Usually everyone thinks of their own region, province, municipality. This is probably a consequence of feeling inadequate to the tasks of life, of withdrawing into oneself to the point of depression and implosion. Now the comparative method can gradually cure the "conditioned reflex" that so readily turns one's own reality into the "exception."

Take, for example, the fine anthology *Cento Sicilie* [A Hundred Sicilies] (1993) by Gesualdo Bufalino and Nunzio Zago, which winds its way through evocative (and savory) passages by writers and social scientists. It undoubtedly endorses the literary spirit and tradition—the poor development of the social sciences may have found some compensation in Sicilian literature, which is extraordinarily fertile. But it is also true that in the anthology the transfiguration of reality (art) ends up prevailing over understanding. The thesis of exceptionalism, however fascinating, creates an arcane, sometimes unfathomable cultural atmosphere that hinders the serene and systematic advancement of thought.[25] Stimuli abound, cognitive theses (on which to base conscious intervention) are scarce.

The key is probably not to be found by rummaging at the bottom of the psychological well of one's own condition (nor by unknowingly mixing it with theories and statistics that do not engage with real life). Breaking free from that mental mold requires following a reverse path—that of taking an interest in other settings, especially Southern, succeeding through comparison (and thus through correspondence and divergence) in better understanding oneself. If the initial self-referential torpor can be overcome; if we observe other situations that have

---

25 This is even more true if in reading these pages we connect them to the tradition of images and stereotypes of the Mezzogiorno (cf. Gribaudi 1989, Dickie 1999 and Moe 1999).

characteristics similar to the one we know, then it will be possible to mentally reduce our own uniqueness by removing them from the dominant position we had previously accorded them, essentially the result of living within a single comparison—between ourselves and the North (and the advanced world in general).

It becomes clear then, *post festum*, that the comparison between the Mezzogiorno and East Germany, as far-fetched as it might have seemed, initially had the merit of serving as an intermediate step in an awareness-raising process. One of its possibilities lies in the fact that since it is a comparison with a distant setting, traditionally regarded as superior but at the same time marked by certain characteristics reminiscent of those known to the Mezzogiorno, it allows Southerners to take a step outside their own intellectual seedbed. Tracing the reasoning in reverse, this explains in part the greater interest of this comparison than others that are possible. It explains how the development of differences, which are indeed multiple, can pave the way for the comparison and thus, by extension, for other comparisons of which we feel the need and urgency.

In other words, once the mystery is discovered, it becomes logical to seize it and turn it to good account. Indeed, the basis of the argument is that we must disengage from a way of seeing the context in which we function as exceptional and at the same time structurally homogeneous (and for that very reason difficult to change). A useful tool in this regard would be an intra-Southern comparison (intra-Mediterranean, intra-Latin, etc.) because this exercise spontaneously produces—more or less quickly and consciously—a process of new acquisitions (including the reinterpretation of what we already knew). Finally, once we become familiar with comparative waters, our navigation can continue on to other shores.[26]

Stefano Ruvolo argued that the title of my 1998 book should have been *On the Side of the Souths* and not *On the Side of the South*. I see in this remark a step forward and perhaps even a healthy rebellion against a culture that has long backed the *forma mentis* referred to above.[27] Undoubtedly, the Mezzogiornos are many — we must not tire of studying them individually, in mutual comparison, in their similar and different characteristics, their positive and negative aspects, and the competitive advantages they possess and could acquire or reinforce. At the same time, we cannot forget that there is a Southern cause, a common cause that is brought into focus precisely by study and comparison.

---

[26] Here I speak from personal experience. Coming from the outside and living in different parts of the South at different times, often overcome by curiosity to understand and the need to do something useful, I ended up spontaneously initiating this work of comparison. If I am not mistaken, this marked the beginning of my personal rupture of the spell of exceptionalism, homogeneity, incomprehensibility and immutability of the Souths and therefore of the South. Hence the need to construct an economic policy that actually responds to the concrete conditions of the different Mezzogiornos and thus concerns itself with their local development.

[27] I am referring to a vast cultural sphere that undoubtedly needs major maintenance — that is, to the economic, historical, philosophical, political, etc. line of thinking that has long spoken *about the* South, *about its* underdevelopment, *about the* Southern question, etc.

THE CHANGE OF IMAGE

4. THE REDISCOVERED MEZZOGIORNO[*]

An Interpretive Hypothesis
1- Which Mezzogiorno are we talking about? Or rather which image of the South does experience suggest that we put forward in order to initiate a new Southern reconnaissance? It is best to come out of our shell and encapsulate our hypothesis in a few schematic points.

(a) It is first and foremost a matter of "seeing and making seen." It is well known that in an apparently normal picture of daily life, the Mezzogiorno suffers from a strong pathological urge that continually crops up at different levels and in different sectors. It was severely aggravated by the interaction between the political system and the population in the declining phase of the First Republic, while the setback it has experienced in recent years has yet to show any sign of turning into a real reversal of the trend. It is a very pernicious disease, the offspring of a rapacious and disruptive present that nevertheless reflects distant historical origins. It is a disease at once individual and social—a characteristic attraction to illegal, clientelist and corporatist behavior incompatible with the creation of a prosperous and modern democratic society with a market economy, as the Southern

[*] From Meldolesi, L. (2022), *Mezzogiorno. Mezzomondo*, pp. 57-70. Originally published in *Sviluppo Locale*, No. 2-3, 1995-1996. I am grateful to the "Artimino gnomes" for giving me the opportunity to discuss passionately some of the ideas contained herein. I also thank Liliana Bàculo, Leonardo Ditta and Nicoletta Stame for suggestions and comments. Finally, I thank the faculty, staff, undergraduates, hundreds of students, not to mention the entrepreneurs, civil servants, and so on whose comments and objections have fostered the maturation of this viewpoint over time. Most of the observations that follow come from my activities in Naples. However, I prefer to focus on the Mezzogiorno because my students come from the various provinces of Campania, Basilicata and Molise, because I have worked in the past in Sicily and Calabria (and am now in contact with Puglia and Abruzzo as well), and because the different societies of the South, although they are autonomous regional entities, are more homogeneous than those of the North and thus lend themselves to more generalizations.

population would desire. It is a pathology that in other guises recurs in other areas of the country as well as abroad.

(b) This pathogenic tendency represents a complex of behaviors available to any individual for achieving his or her own goals — alternative to the legitimate ones of work, merit, and the democratic formation of political consensus. It manifests itself in a thousand different guises — from the most heinous crimes to the myriad forms of scheming — as a partly illegal, partly legal (or legalized) phenomenon that can be differentiated into "three scourges": crime (or criminality), clientelism and corporatism.[1] Its strength is such that, as recent "rankings" unfortunately show, it is not only the South, but the whole of Italy that at times takes on the characteristic of a semi-corrupt and semi-criminal country.

(c) Thus, the disease besieges Italian society in the South from all sides. All local communities in the South are forced to tolerate it. Many are so afflicted that they take on a broken-down, disorganized and distressed appearance. Like a plant overwhelmed by parasites, productive and civic life in these places, unable to respond adequately, is forced to adapt. Elsewhere, this leaves the field to extraordinarily varied forms of disarray and connivance, while in still other areas these are fortunately episodic or even absent. No wonder, then, that between civilized and pathological behavior a wide intermediate zone of intermixing and confusion has been created that tends to swing alternately in one direction or the other.

(d) In this continuous undertow, opposition movements often lose their bearings, and in opposing perhaps one of the scourges they end up aligning themselves with another. This way, resistance efforts (which in order to be effective become

---

[1] See Meldolesi, L. "The Three Scourges", in Stame, N., ed., (2024) *An Education*, the first book in this trilogy of "Selected writings by Luca and Friends".

radicalized) can themselves easily take on a corporatist, clientelist and even criminal appearance. But the three scourges, while distinct, are interconnected — part of a single pathology.[2] This suggests that the conscientious opponent should assume an attitude that is at once rigorous and flexible — capable of punctually intervening in an anti-pathological key by intelligently enhancing positive processes, whatever social and political form they may take. This is a delicate and complex job that requires a good dose of "possibilist" training.

(e) The pathology of the Mezzogiorno attacks productive businesses on a daily basis and firmly occupies, at different levels, a significant share of local institutions. It casts a sinister shadow over the entire life of the country. With four seriously infected regions (Campania, Puglia, Calabria and Sicily) and one endangered (Sardinia), with a central administration largely paralyzed by parasitism and corruption, and with pathological offshoots spreading in every direction, the nation is unable to play the role of "protagonist of reason" that, however, would be within its reach. This gives the Southern question a new and decisive relevance for our future — a very different role from the traditional one.

(f) If we look closely at the circumstances of production in Southern local systems, it is possible to appreciate the nefarious function of the disease. While contextual, tacit knowledge in North-Central local systems is given value by supplementing it with codified, predominantly imported knowledge, the overall inhospitable environment for productive activities in

---

[2] The citizen's impoverished imagination generally keeps the three spheres of crime, clientele and corporation separate. But the very serious instances of intermixing in recent years have forced many to reconsider. "Paraphrasing the Crocian lesson of the circularity of the human Spirit," wrote a witty witness (Luca Torre. Introduction to M. Serao, 1994, p. LXI), "we should perhaps have taken into account that nexus which binds the various forms of the Spirit."

many South-Central settings generates an attitude of underestimation and sometimes even contempt for local skills that are often linked in memory to the "toil" of the recent past—the craftsman, the farmer, the fisherman. While in the North-Center, cooperation among enterprises tempers their competition, here the lack of mutual trust in business practices severely hinders local development. While in other parts of the country the sense of identification with the fate of the enterprise and more generally with local affairs counterbalances conflicts of interest (up to a point), in the South "shortsightedness" and proud and disruptive individualism lead many industries (especially public) to disintegrate.

(g) In the North-Center, furthermore, local governments often turn into centers of initiative that can provide efficient services to the productive base and support modernization and restructuring processes in various ways. In the South, on the other hand, private use of public assets and offices is unfortunately common currency. Public services for industry and industrial policy are very sluggish—sometimes they are conspicuous in their absence, when they are not causing actual harm (as for example in the case of political kickbacks demanded in exchange for normal duties). More generally, the recent major pathological epoch in the South has left deep scars in all local governments (starting with the regions). It is now a question of climbing back up the slope. The law on the direct election of mayors, by creating personal responsibility and legitimacy, has (for once) played a positive role. But from here the step to satisfactory local politics in symbiosis with the people is a long one, not least because it would require the gradual breakup of the illegal, clientelist and corporatist forces that lurk in the administration and political leadership. I do not believe that such a step can be accomplished by some cinematic "special effect," such as that claimed by some for "fiscal federalism."

(h) Fortunately, however, the picture outlined is not homogeneous. The "great transformation" of the 1950s and 60s affected the entire territory, generating an agricultural exodus, urbanization and emigration. The resulting local systems present a variety of conditions that we are still well short of having brought under control. If we compare it with Manlio Rossi-Doria's well-known tri-partition of the South into mountains, hills and plains, we can see that the current situation does not bend to the logic of bone and flesh — which would give the lowlands an advantage in terms of industrialization. Instead, areas with different states of development coexist, especially in the hills and the plains, both as a result of the different historical and human "endowments" of the relative communities, and because of the highly dissimilar degree of their respective pathologies. Hence therefore the need for a comparative study of local systems in the South (and North as well) from which to learn in detail the lessons of their developmental paths.

(i) By way of illustration, there are in the Mezzogiorno productive nuclei that are in full development — at the center of local systems differing in location and size that are often "encircled" by everything else. There are also areas where the development of local systems is more conflicted and intermittent, and others where widespread development potential is kept in check and depleted by the pathologies mentioned above. Finally, there are areas where the pathology has taken over, effectively replacing legitimate authorities and imposing its law. On the whole, it can be said that judging by the capacities that exist and the results that have been achieved, the industrial potential of many areas does not appear qualitatively different from what has flourished in other parts of the country.

(j) If we then get even more specific, we have to recognize that the most culturally endowed and populous areas are generally not the ones that have been successful — the pathological tendencies and political clout of these areas seem to clash dramatically with their historical legacy. In contrast, some less populous and more secluded areas have emerged that would almost like to recognize themselves as outside the Southern quagmire.[3] As for local skills, then, those of everyday artisans: the carpenter, the tailor, the shoemaker, and their cultured counterparts: silk, cameo, artistic pottery, etc. are both in the process of partial enhancement. This connective tissue includes the remnants of past experiences of industrialization, as well as the new and important introduction of domestic and foreign businesses from the various industrial sectors.

(k) It is therefore not true that the Mezzogiorno is "underdeveloped." What *is* true is that its society is sick and therefore in pain. The Italian South is no longer (predominantly) agricultural and is not just on welfare. Again, the production of goods and services is predominant and widespread, but unfortunately it is daily kept in check and partly stifled. It is an industrialization that is widespread but fragile, composed mainly of medium-sized, small and tiny enterprises that have to defend themselves daily against repeated sniping by various authorities (institutional, administrative, repressive, criminal, trade union etc.) and more generally against behavior incompatible with the orderly conduct of business. For these reasons, businesses tend to "close in" on themselves, to develop the art of legal-fiscal cosmetics, to look for subterranean channels of dubious "regularity" even with regard to labor, and to lower their profile to the point of hiding in the folds of society and the territory. This is the "cloaked business".

---

[3] For example, the people of Irpinia do not feel Neapolitan, while Molisans and Lucanians look to Umbria, Marche and Tuscany. It is a desire for "standardization" that in the more enterprising areas aims to adopt "Third Italy" behavior, while in the more backward areas it translates into simple fairy-tale admiration: "there you could live well."

(l) But this is not necessarily a "third-tier" or marginal situation. The local capabilities mentioned earlier also relate to significant companies, some of them leaders in market segments. Yet the overall context pushes even these companies toward defensive and camouflaging behavior. Moreover, the condition of subservience in which so many productive activities in the South are forced to live leaves the field open to a range of professions functioning as mediators and representatives with respect to the pathological drive—open, that is, to corporatism and clientelism as well as spontaneous and organized lawlessness. Lawyers, high-level bureaucrats, notaries, etc. continue to have a role of disproportionate prestige in Mezzogiorno townships that otherwise would not be justified.

(m) The conclusion, then, is that the everyday visual impression of the Mezzogiorno is basically true, although it needs to be carefully decoded. I am thinking of the very extensive (and somewhat Americanized) average imitative consumption that goes hand in hand with the reluctance to declare amounts and forms of income—especially of productive income. I am thinking of the undervaluing of manual labor and entrepreneurial labor, of the attractiveness of collecting rent, of the stable job, of being "settled." And of the desire to get rich without "toil." It is this environment that we must change through iterative processes that privilege and gradually strengthen the reality of Southern labor, intermittently involving different levels and forces in the Mezzogiorno and the country as a whole.

The Metaphor of the Journey

2 – I don't know how the reader will react to this image of the Mezzogiorno. I suspect that in the South it will appear too stark and, in the North, too emotional. However, its deliberately schematic construction should not hide the arduous journey that produced it, which included involving other people

and fortunately finding a more expeditious pace. *Ab initio* I should perhaps contextualize the decision I made when I began to work in the Mezzogiorno. My aim was shoulder my responsibilities in the face of the country's greatest problem, and therefore to press ahead with a pursuit that had long appeared fruitless.[4] What happened instead was that perspectives and interpretive concepts tested and re-tested *ad nauseam* in observation and dialogue with friends and students[5] ended up finding their own grounding so as to serve as a basis for further acquisitions.

Here, then, the metaphor of the journey of discovery of the Mezzogiorno finds a certain relevance. It helps us make the case that Mezzogiorno is a little-known reality, intricate and complex, and that in order not to lose our bearings it is wise to follow a north star—the public interest.[6] It helps us see that understanding the South requires an effort "outside the box," which

---

[4] It is as if I had taken on the role of Micco Macco the Explorer, the protagonist of a little song from my childhood who "searches, searches and what does he find? Four python eggs.... And the four little pythons go away with four little bows."

[5] I am referring to the research work on the Mezzogiorno over the past ten years coordinated at successive times by Liliana Baculo, Paolo Di Nola, Luca Meldolesi, Gianni Molinari and Nicoletta Stame at the Department of Economic and Social Sciences at the University of Naples.

[6] Interest in the "common good," a sense of the state and of public morality are indispensable reference points for the present research. Rather than in a legal-philosophical sense, they should be understood in an economic-social sense, and with a concrete policy angle. This is not to be confused with a curious mental archetype present in the Mezzogiorno, according to which one *should* of course behave impeccably, but since such behavior "is not of this world"... many things become permissible. At the very least (as I don't tire of repeating) someone who steals an apple or fails to pay a streetcar fare cannot be compared to Broccoletti and Poggiolini [egregious public managers in the Ministry of Health, convicted of bribery within the "Clean Hands" campaign]. One should not get stuck at every turn chasing a misguided need for absolutes—instead, one's general orientation and behavior should be clear and consistent. The public interest—and with it the collective need to consolidate and develop a truly democratic market-economy society in the South--must prevail over political choices. Indeed, the southern condition is so difficult that, in my opinion, political forces can become agents of change in the desired direction only if they know how to put the public interest

entails a crossing of disciplinary barriers and the use of multiple methodologies.[7] It also clarifies my need to work "at street level," repeatedly questioning the phenomena encountered, and not backing away even in the face of their acutely abhorrent nature. Of course, I am not about to re-enact this trajectory. Rather, I would like to recall some aspects of it in order to make the hypothesis sketched out above more understandable.

The view from the North and the Center of the country offers no awareness of the severity and extent of the "Italian disease," which is on the contrary palpable in the South. Most people lack direct experience of its acute forms, and this makes it less easy to decode the common ones that are widespread in our native habitat (and which sadly sit comfortably with many people). Together with the wholly Southern need to underestimate the phenomenon in order to be able to maintain "hope," this creates a murky atmosphere which, although at times torn by pathological outbreaks and scandals, is nevertheless a serious obstacle to the process of rehabilitation. One way to overcome this state of collective consciousness is to acclimatize one's vision to the criminal reality of the South and then mentally reconstruct the contours of the overall phenomenon of the "three scourges." This requires no more than an act of will that surmounts current attitudes, such as "épater la bourgeoisie" or the cunning of the couch-potato reason. In fact, there is nothing mysterious about the subject. In a very short time one can learn a great deal about a distinct, diverse, and constantly evolving environment, which unfortunately assaults and drains the social fabric in so many parts of southern Italy. I can say that it was actually my students who propelled me in this direction—

---

before their tactical choices (and thus indirectly validate their popular legitimacy).
[7] I am referring here to my long work with and on Fernand Braudel and Albert Hirschman, who has been the indispensable companion of the "new hypotheses" concerning the South.

through detailed reconstructions of what was going on in their own areas.

In the years of triumphant (and complicit) clientelism this concrete observation had the great virtue of opening my eyes. It drew a clear line of demarcation and also suggested some elements of an anti-pathogenic economic policy that could clear a path among the pitfalls laid out by the recognized schools of thought. For some time, the process of exploring the disease and generalizing about it, and that of finding concrete solutions mutually reinforced each other—even today their progress continues.[8] They created by degrees an unprecedented viewpoint which, linked up with other inputs, showcased additional possibilities. This is the process that has allowed us to "rediscover" the Mezzogiorno.

In retrospect, it makes sense to me that this occurred as a result of the negative aspect of the analysis meeting the positive aspect found in the field. I am referring here to the research on youth entrepreneurship in the Mezzogiorno coordinated by Paolo Di Nola and Nicoletta Stame, the study of a group of successful cases coordinated by Liliana Bàculo, and the hunt for businesses launched by Gianni Molinari. All three cases resulted in the discovery of a Mezzogiorno that asserts itself despite the disease. The study of about fifty companies of youth

---

[8] Indeed, although I had spoken far and wide about criminality and clientelism, probably because of my background I had not mustered the strength to propose corporatism as the "third scourge." It was the absurd "battle" of Petrobras in Brazil and President Cardoso's reference to clientelism and corporatism as "demons" to be kept in check that hit home with me, suggesting the present locution. As for the economic policy proposals, the path of systematization and articulation that began with *Mezzogiorno, con gioia* [Mezzogiorno with Joy] (1990) and continued with *Come sospingere il Mezzogiorno verso l'Europa* [How to Push the Mezzogiorno Toward Europe] (1994a), *I cento gamberi* [The Hundred Shrimps] (1996b) and *Uno schema per il Sud* [A Scheme for the South] (1996c) [see, ch. 7 of this volume] continues to make progress. Unfortunately, the parallel path of exploring policymaking from this point of view (Meldolesi, 1994b, Ch. 4) is still in the experimental stage.

entrepreneurship—Law 44/1986, the only part of the Intervento Straordinario per il Mezzogiorno that survived its demise—showed in great detail that this happened because (initially, at least) the experiment was carefully constructed and managed (to a large extent) with a series of anti-clientelist and anti-corporatist arrangements.[9] Moreover, the cases of industrial success identified by Liliana's collective along with the many others found later alerted us to a vast and important— and largely underestimated—world.

Here further paths began to emerge. The first of these regarded products and related skills which, as might have been expected, struggle *harder* in the Mezzogiorno to find a road to development.[10] Other survey data on greater verticalization of enterprises (i.e. on the reduced exploitation of external economies) and on the insufficient social cohesion inside and outside firms allowed us to complete the picture—and thus to find a *trait-d'union* with the "philosophy of the "district" experts. The possibility opened up of studying the interweaving of the three "scourges" and the three "fundamental balances" developed by that philosophy as the logical-historical *pendant* of productive techniques, of competition and social conflict—well-known aspects of economic life. It is thus clear that our interest in the literature on districts and small businesses in the North-Center had nothing contrived about it—it did not spring from a desire for a mechanical transposition of those experiences to the South. On the contrary, it was the study of our own world

---

[9] Cf. Di Nola, 2000; Meldolesi and Stame, 1995.

[10] "And note," wrote Matilde Serao a century ago (now in 1994, p. 17), "that the elegant young people are the best dressed in Italy, that the most beautiful shoes and the finest affordable furniture are made in Naples, and that Naples produces the best gloves." It is worth mentioning how I came into contact with this issue. Some years ago, an employee of my department asked me if I wanted him to make me a jacket. I later found out that he was a tailor who had been preyed upon in the past by the Camorra and had to emigrate and that in Milan he had become a janitor....

that led us in stages to this rendezvous. Fortunately, the "hiding hand" (of Hirschmanian memory) concealed from us some of the difficulties. Thus (and despite some slip-ups), an unprecedented channel of communication was set in motion between different parts of the country — one that we hope to consolidate and develop in different directions.

This also appears significant from a second point of view. Indeed, our work had already given rise to a "territorial dispute." The highly varied and surprising location of the industrial centers that had been identified prompted a critical comparison with the territorial generalizations of Manlio Rossi-Doria (and with the mid-1960s dialogue on the Mezzogiorno between him and Albert Hirschman). This paved the way for the forthcoming study of Southern local systems. Not to mention, lastly, the direct election of some "honest" mayors (including Maurizio Maturo in Mugnano di Napoli), which has created new space for the gradual strengthening of our perspective.

If this is indeed the case, one final point remains to be clarified. This is whether it is possible to construct a reasonable "snapshot" of the contemporary Mezzogiorno, amenable (of course) to enlargements, retouches and modifications in its various parts. If it is indeed possible to place it usefully in contact with formulations relating to other parts of the country in the perspective of a broader understanding, why have we had to live up to now in relative seclusion? Why have these ideas not even been considered by so-called Meridionalism?

Of course there are reasons of education, of professional interest and of a subjective nature that partly explain this state of affairs. But it is also true that well-meaning Northerners coming to the South encounter an opaque and scattered socio-economic culture that, with a few exceptions, does not have much to say about either the pathological side or the positive, industrial side of conditions in the South. It simply does not take the trouble, this culture, to get to know these things first-hand because it does not consider it necessary. Yet it endures over time, a sign that it has its own internal strength and functions effectively.

On the other hand, we spoke earlier about a certain confusion and fragmentation of the collective scene, and the mediating and agency roles played by traditional professional figures that are much less significant elsewhere. We must now add that the diseased sector of Southern society, in its various criminal, clientelist and corporate articulations, brings into play substantial local forces that are always alert in the hope of finding ways to "feed" themselves and the vast professional and popular area connected to them. For this reason, they are spontaneously interested in any form of bulkhead, argumentation or representation that might play into their hands.[11]

For example, for funding that comes from the European Union, the blueprint is set. It is just a matter of staying informed and identifying any possible room for maneuver (perhaps "setting aside" initiatives that do not contain any). But as far as Italian funds are concerned, things are different. Here at every rustling of the bushes from the North or from Rome, the game is set in motion in the hope of widening the "opening" that has just been glimpsed. From this point of view, it is in no one's interest (to say the least) that we go and see how things actually are in the South — the findings would be somewhat embarrassing. Instead, it is necessary to beat the drum for the

---

[11] This is part of an even larger phenomenon and implies a process of substantial adaptation and hence of subordination. A large part of the South, more than deciding what it wants, has the problem of taking the "right side" so as to have a say about the "spoils" that will follow. Once the game plays out, this group, often referred to by the misnomer "rent party," will find a modus vivendi that will allow it to perpetuate itself and, if possible, prosper. Thus, for example, the South has grudgingly "adapted" to the "constructivist" phase of the European Community and will no doubt also adapt to the newly opened "German" phase based on principles of mutual recognition and subsidiarity.

neglected South, to put forward credible arguments for getting "distributable" money flowing, to strengthen the parliamentary lobby, etc. To this end, anything goes. Indeed, it makes sense, where possible, to support other points of view, from the North, say, that leave some room free — as long as they carry weight and bring coverage.

Yet, after the shakeup of recent years, it must be pointed out that there is something new under the sun today. Perhaps the self-reference of the Northern regions[12] and the pathogenic pressure coming from the South are no longer so dominant. In the North, especially in Emilia, there is an economic-social diffusion process, while in the South the new economic reality is timidly trying to come forward. The very fact of having finally come across both the one and the other can be interpreted as a reason for reasonable hope. This, for encouragement if nothing else, is my "prophecy."

---

[12] By self-reference I mean here a mobilizing and cumulative effort within local systems by a region that has little confidence in its own external projection. This was the case for the "red regions" in the postwar period that faced central Christian Democrat power. Later it was the case of the "League" areas and especially the Triveneto. But just as in the theory of territorial development, alongside processes of polarization, diffusive processes have always existed which also affect the country's political landscape, and these are currently experiencing renewed development.

5. Initial Ideas for the Local Development of the Mezzogiorno*

1 – An ex-student of mine who became the mayor of a town in the Neapolitan hinterland forced to go around with an armed escort. Three ironic articles—actually meant to intimidate—that appeared in a financial newspaper under a pseudonym that reportedly hid the former viceroy of Naples, Paolo Cirino Pomicino. An attitude of disquiet, not to say contempt, toward small businesses, which meanders among teachers, civil servants, administrators, big industrialists, and professional circles, all lined up in defense of their *formae mentis* – traditional "welfarism" and corporate prerogatives. In the late summer, the "three scourges"[1] show up for the appointment. I greet them with mixed feelings. First of all, it would be difficult to find more convincing evidence in the real world than what I originally wrote for Artimino '95—namely, that the Southern reality is deeply furrowed by the contextual presence of both positive and pathogenic behaviors. Those who wish to develop this duality in a constructive direction must know that they are drawing to themselves the attention of the powers behind the

---

* From: Meldolesi, L. (2020), *Montagne russe. Italia Vulcanica*, n. 6-7, pp. 70-110. The present paper does not follow the route that the "Artiminian" reader would expect. Privileging local analysis and intervention in the Mezzogiorno should not mean burdening it with those economic policy responsibilities that can be addressed, with any perspective, only if they are broken down and attacked from other sides as well. For this reason, while using the local level as a constant reference point, our discourse strives to build a broader framework in order to gradually push it in the direction of local development. Out of this these "first ideas" arise, from which, if the experience takes root, more specific reasoning may follow. "The elucidation of immediate experience is the sole justification for any thought; and the starting point for thought is the analytic observation of components of this experience." The following pages have also drawn encouragement from this maxim of Whitehead's.
[1] Cf. Meldolesi, L. (1998a): part. 1, ch. 2. As "The Three Scourges" it appears in Stame, N., ed. (2024), the first book in this trilogy of "Selected Writings of Luca and Friends."

disease—very different from each other perhaps, but unfortunately convergent, linked through multiple equilibria, and objectively interconnected.

Readers will find meager consolation in this, especially if they are prone to the kind of Southern pessimism that paves the way for acquiescence. This is a useful observation because, taken together with the previous one, it delimits the logical field that the following pages fit into. In the face of such a difficult reality—I do not tire of repeating—we need not choose between the behavior of the lion and that of the sheep, a very common procedure.[2] Rather, it is a matter of extricating ourselves from the exceptional nature of the one and the everyday quality of the other. It is about developing an acute perception of the actually existing possibility of escaping this antinomy and operating effectively.

The Setting

2 – While representing—we should keep in mind—about half of Italy's territory and population, the Central-Southern part of the country remains largely unstudied.[3] Thus, during the past year,

---

[2] From the outside, it is difficult to realize how criminal violence also serves the purpose of reaffirming typical sequences of subjugation that continue to regulate a very wide arc of social relations. A marginal but illuminating example of this came to me from a student. His father had left his car in a no parking zone next to many others. On returning, he noticed that only his had been ticketed, while the others belonged to shopkeepers who had "settled" with the police. He thus decided to report the matter to the judiciary. But while awaiting trial he received an avalanche of steep fines that led him to withdraw the complaint. As can be seen, following established social trajectories, power relations polluted by pathogenic relations take the place here of the legal functioning of collective life. In reacting to the abuse—as I explained to the student—his father had erred twice. Firstly, because in following his own individual pride, he had not appreciated the strength of his opponent's reaction—things would have been different if the complaint had been collective. And secondly because, having been targeted, he had seen no alternative but to return to the fold.

[3] Indeed, indirect research based on statistics prevails, while the few field surveys struggle to find their way to reasonable generalizations. This is probably a consequence of the implosive trend of which we shall say more below. See also n. 21.

finding ourselves in a situation of (unintentional) near-monopoly, my collaborators and I have sought a visual angle more in keeping with expectations. Mainly through the students in the course we resumed and explored further our dialogue with several provinces in the continental Mezzogiorno, while at the same time, focusing our attention on the Grumo Nevano quadrilateral (or Atellan quadrilateral, from the city of Atella that once dominated the area[4]). This dual observation gradually gave rise to a further fine-tuning of Southern problems and their "intractability." In short, we found abundant grist for our mill.

As a first step, to acclimatize the eyes and enter the labyrinth, it is worthwhile to invoking the visual impressions that accompany the visitor on any Southern journey. I will try to organize them from three points of view: legality-illegality, private-public, and that of light industrialization.

A society that is above board exists in the Mezzogiorno only on the surface. The inclination to widespread illegality is present in many parts of the country (remember "Clean Hands"); but in its intense form, it is specific to the South—it represents almost a conditioned reflex through which the question is not so much whether an act is more or less legitimate, but whether it goes (concretely) against a specific sanction. "Here it is the law of the 'poker face' that applies," a privileged witness told me, for example, to explain the rampant occurrence of under-invoicing.

This mental attitude, though very different from area to area and between hills and plains, permeates the Mezzogiorno thoroughly and manifests itself in a thousand different aspects

---

[4] In and around this quadrilateral that stretches north of Naples between the city and the Autostrada del Sole, more than half a million people circulate. The area, now prey to a peculiar form of automobile culture, is built on a whole series of earlier societies. In particular, the distribution of land to Roman soldiers is clearly visible in the Aversano in the striking "grid layout" of a substantial part of the territory.

that are not easy to evaluate and generalize. For example, those who emphasize the presence of organized crime often end up exaggerating it and thereby preclude a realistic perception of everyday life. Moreover, the geography of crime is highly diverse — crime-family rule is one thing, gang warfare is another, a third is "protection," a fourth is petty crime, and so on. Not to mention, finally, that the specifics of crimes must be kept in mind, along with their degree of severity and the impact they come to have on the social context.

At the same time, recorded criminal activities are unfortunately a small part of what actually takes place.[5] Many crimes go unreported, and many others go undetected (e.g., acts of corruption). Beyond crimes against the person, the illegality extends into the vast field of dealings with the authorities. Finally, the *propensity* for illegality is even more vast, including all those practices — obstructive, bureaucratic, parasitic, etc. — that are not properly illegal, but which interfere with the normal course of social life.

In short, our visitor's first visual (and true) impression is that southern society is double-faced, with illegal behavior (with varying degrees of illegality) on one side, and legal behavior on the other — and somewhere between the two, there is tolerated illegal behavior (of many kinds) and behavior that is only formally legal. Only a small part of society lives in a condition of full legality — without resorting even to market manipulation through inside information, petty corruption, etc. It generally does this as an unspoken challenge to the current trend, for reasons of point-scoring and as an aspiration to a more civilized life.

---

[5] According to an opinion poll by IPR Marketing (1996, p. 4), 29 percent of Neapolitan citizens claim to have been victims of a mugging, theft or robbery in the past year.

The first lesson therefore comes from them. Anyone who intends to engage in the Mezzogiorno must operate in full legality by developing pliant tactics that can discriminate in the sea of illegality with the intention of changing things—avoiding, as mentioned above, the errors of submissiveness and head-on confrontation.[6]

3 – A second and long noted key aspect of the Southern world has been given different appellations over time, such as amoral family values, lack of civic sense, *maladie d'amour*, insufficiency of relational assets, and so on. It is basically a marked asymmetry in favor of the private sphere (individual and family)— a tendency exacerbated by the structural asymmetry that divides the country and more generally by the asymmetry between the private and public characteristic of market societies.[7]

One need only look at the homes of the Southern lower-middle class.[8] Immediately apparent is the great effort put into

---

[6] Even the great Giovanni Falcone—to whose work for the emancipation of the Mezzogiorno Marco Chiauzzi is dedicating his dissertation—can be criticized in this regard. The very high personal risk Falcone took by bravely waging war on the Mafia was not compatible with his habit of traveling to Palermo to see his wife, Francesca. Moreover, seeking out the path between "sheep" behavior and "lion" behavior makes sense even from a private point of view. A person "in the cross-hairs" of criminality must navigate between the two dangers. If the menace comes from a group of delinquents, the vigilance of law enforcement might be the best option. But, if the threat is serious, extricating oneself may require exploiting the adversary's weaknesses, such as provincialism and shortsightedness. Since the criminal group will want to act right away, the best option is to vanish. As often happens, the group will most likely shift its attentions somewhere else.

[7] Actually, the obsessive comparison with the North that encapsulates Southern life results first and foremost in the desire to consume like the North (as seen on television)—at level of consumption that leaves no room for savings. This reduces families' latitude for protection and planning. Moreover, such obsessive self-referencing leads to an underestimation of local opportunities, especially of a public nature.

[8] I have in mind those who send their children to college: teachers, white-collar workers, professionals, small businessmen, merchants, laborers, farmers, etc. As (probably) one of the few teachers who maintains relationships with families, I have had the opportunity to visit numerous apartments. I learned a lot from such

achieving a level of income and consumption considered acceptable (target income). The apartment, often the aspiration of a lifetime and generally oversized relative to the needs of a nuclear family of four or five people, is modernized at regular intervals and is full of light, and brightly polished by a female hand, with particular attention to the bathroom and kitchen. In short, it is a realm of domestic tranquility that contrasts, even visually, with an external reality which, while lively, is also chaotic and disorganized. People's best face is turned towards the family, even to the point of (paradoxically) justifying external practices that are anything but commendable. Thus, the dual nature of Southern society comes to the fore yet again.

Nuclear families are connected to each other by kinship and friendship. Toward third parties they generally assume an attitude of short-term self-interest. Private purposes are gratified socially, while very little energy is devoted to the public interest. Contradicting Blaise Pascal, the people of the South would claim to expect politicians to be angels, but actually believe they are beasts serving their own self-interest.

The public sphere is widely viewed with skepticism (and often even moral condemnation). This pushes individuals to retreat to the private sphere—here alone they feel in control. It is from this sense of inadequacy (and more generally because of the often-difficult external economic life) that the propensity towards guile and lawlessness in the end arises.

What can be done then in such an uninviting landscape? How to combat the blatant large-scale building speculation that is routinely condoned, the unraveling of public entities used for private purposes, and the trend toward even visual degradation and decay? First and foremost, we must not be discouraged. Next, the public interest must be placed above

---

wanderings, especially in the Campania hinterland because there most basic observation is captured at root level.

any partisan choice. And finally, ways must be found to employ intelligent tactics to harness the swings in favor of collective interests that may exist on the local level — all the while aware, however, that the undertow will bring with it much unpleasantness.

4 – Finally, we come to the third key aspect chosen to introduce the reader to contemporary Southern society — the trend toward light industrialization. This is a little-known (and little-recognized) characteristic. For many years it moved with soft steps, unwittingly protected by the public's pitying attitude toward it. Small businesses in South Italy have long been considered marginal, subsistence activities, doomed to a very short life cycle.[9]

Yet, we need only adjust our eyes to the subterranean light to realize that in many Southern settings there is a swarm of small-scale enterprises, true vitality, an intense hive of activity that is channeled — directly and indirectly — into the mobilization of goods for highways and ports — and now railways as well. This network of activities has its own points of aggregation and many avenues of dispersal. Reconstructing its history generally reveals that a small entrepreneur "stumbled upon" the right move at the right time and was quickly followed by others, thereby revealing a local vocation that has since been consolidated.

Having opened the way for market success, the local environment reacted with a vigorous mobilization of latent capabilities and hidden resources, developing a cluster of enterprises linked together by an incipient interrelationship. This

---

[9] The ideological grip of the "pessimistic view" (of which more below) has kept us from looking deeper into these approximate generalizations — and determining whether, for example, the numerous births and deaths of businesses (a key element of the so-called turbulence thesis) are often part of a tax evasion gimmick (Meldolesi, 1995, p. 37-38).

embryo of a local system began to spread out, dispensing its beneficial effects to the fullest and assembling a "strike force" capable of invading the market.[10] This is the pattern of local mini-booms that spring up in the hills and in the plains, modifying the landscape and inducing haphazard urbanization and building speculation.

Looking at the merchandise, we find ourselves for the most part in the classic household and personal goods category. Of course, some of these products are standardized and in competition with goods from the third world and therefore pay starvation wages. But this is not the prevailing condition — even in the Mezzogiorno, among the thousand products of light industry, the "limited edition" and the "premium price" are prevalent, linked to know-how, product innovation, and the ability to react to often quirky market trends. As a result, wages for undeclared work are not far from (or trend towards) minimum wages. It is this South — as far as I can tell — which accounts for the relative resilience of Southern income and consumption, despite the economic situation — the suspension of the Intervento Straordinario, the "containment" of ordinary spending, the collapse and restructuring of public enterprise, the withdrawal of many multinationals, etc.

5 – It is here, then, that our question comes to the fore. The small Southern business is in the global game with the rest of the world. 70-80% of its output is destined for markets in the

---

[10] Illuminating in this regard is Sara Gaudino's (1998) reconstruction of the emergence of the swimwear industry in the Gragnano area and its sudden success in the market. This may happen in the case of the most upscale sectors — think of the highest quality clothing firms. But the "foot soldiers" of the process seem to focus on mid-range and medium-low range products that are able to penetrate markets, foreign included, by offering acceptable substitutes for existing goods, but at sharply lower prices. Natuzzi, for example, by "obliterating" the unit price has captured twenty percent of the US leather sofa market.

North-Central zone and abroad. The relationships between owner accounts and third-party accounts, while varying from one area to another, do not seem substantially different from those existing elsewhere (and do not therefore lend themselves to easy generalizations).[11] On the contrary, it is logical that in a general condition in which the same commodity originates from very different production processes, the small Southern industry will try to make the most of its positive cards and neutralize the negative ones.

In fact, behind such successes it is not difficult to glimpse first and foremost a focus on the private individual. Typically, a small business relies on a group of friends and relatives linked to the entrepreneur by long-standing familiarity. It is this group that contains the essential skills of planning, organizing, producing, financing and protecting the enterprise. This group is always "on call" — it lives with the company and delivers impressive flexibility and quantity and quality of work. Its roots may be found in inter-family relationships. Here the sense of belonging is born that binds individuals to the enterprise, and with it the pride of building something important.[12]

Moreover, behind these successes arising spontaneously from below (often thanks to manual workers from other backgrounds) there is a freedom of movement that has without scruple taken advantage of the full range of opportunities — including, of course, the circumvention of tax and labor legislation (Meldolesi 1996a; Meldolesi, Arbitrio, Del Monaco, 1996).

---

[11] Of course, this is not to deny the differences that exist in terms of capital strength, access to credit, administrative and commercial organization, etc., which correspond to the different levels of industrialization in different parts of the country. Moreover, it should be pointed out that the sector was largely external to the "grand tourbillon " of financing for the Mezzogiorno during First Republic.

[12] Including, of course, the potential shame of failing (the scuorno) and thus losing social respectability (Meldolesi, 1998a, p. 89). So that entrepreneurial risk (which in a family business is normally tinged with emotional distress) here reaches an unusual level of intensity.

Hypotheses and Ferment

6 - Southern light industrialization thus operates—how could it be otherwise?—from within particular collective psychological structures that in part differ from those existing elsewhere. Businesses—to exemplify—progressively find their economic equilibrium and capacity for expansion by exploiting the compactness of the reference group, drawing on undeclared labor, or taking advantage of the absence of the administration. But of course, there is a flip side to this coin, as we shall now see.

In discussing the problem of local action, I argued above that it must operate in full legality and promote the gradual legalization of collective life, seeking a flexible tactic that can take advantage of the avenues of the possible. These are general principles that clearly presuppose the hypothesis, or wager if you like—that Southern light industrialization has partly exhausted its little subterranean ultra-individualist *Sturm und Drang* and is gradually becoming open to a change of direction.

Could not its productive forces, to put it the old-fashioned way, benefit from a partial modification of the relations of production? This *demodé* question does not seem misplaced. It is probably what underlies a series of phenomena that have occurred in recent years in the opinions of young people, and in Southern culture, politics and social forces.[13] But, precisely because of its importance, this wager must first of all be protected from us—that is, from our spontaneous tendency, anthropomorphic in origin, to superimpose our individual and collective desires on an understanding of reality (Colorni, 1975).

---

[13] Among other things, it would help interpret the collective experience at the heart of the present work. (I hasten also to point out that, unlike what was thought in the past, the hypothesis proposed here of the interrelation between the economy—productive forces—and social and political phenomena—relations of production—places these elements on a plane of absolute parity).

That is also why I will try to examine it from different perspectives.

7 – The first of these might be to look at the South from beyond its borders. The opportunity to do so is provided by a recent event that concerns me. In the fall of 1995, invigorated by participation in Artimino, I undertook to write an essay on the high labor mobility in the Atellan quadrilateral.[14] I thought I should send a copy to Bruno Contini, one of my main interlocutors. He discussed it with Mario Pirani and phoned me and asked me to send a copy to him as well. Thus began an episode that had many surprises in store.

Pirani wrote an initial article in *La Repubblica* that remains probably the most lucid of the entire campaign.[15] At first it seemed that the thing was not destined to last, and it was only later that a small group of journalists formed around us. The point is that, as a research group we were now able to argue with full knowledge of the existence of a widespread proclivity for light industrialization in the Mezzogiorno—and we could also rely on a network of students in the field, able to prepare

[14] This study (Meldolesi, Arbitrio, Del Monaco 1996), which benefited from the contribution of two outstanding research assistants, Angela Arbitrio and Mariabrigida Del Monaco, was commissioned to me by the Confindustria Studies Office as part of a study of mobility in Italian society. Years ago, I had discussed my research on the South with Gianpaolo Galli, then a Bank of Italy official. Having become head of the Confindustria Studies Office he evidently thought that my empirical curiosity was useful in decoding the "mystery" of labor mobility in the Mezzogiorno.

[15] Pirani called my essay "a document surprising for its novelty, to be read like travelogues in unknown lands used to be (...) Out of it emerges unexpectedly a 'path of hope' toward the creation of a society based on a market economy even in the Mezzogiorno. An intuition (...) supported by 'discoveries' that seem to echo those of modern historiographical archaeology, which by analyzing layers of soil and shards is capable of finding and studying the historical relics of earlier complex civilizations. In our case, researchers have devoted themselves to a veritable 'hunt for businesses down the block.' "Isn't it perhaps time," concluded Pirani, "that we journalists, too, set off again to discover Italy, instead of wasting time in the bushes?" For once—it is safe to say—this question from one of the of the doyens of Italian journalism has not fallen on deaf ears.

for the journalists' visit and thus enable them to get an idea first-hand of the living reality of things.

Our studies and formulations on the South had now found a public outlet we hadn't dreamed of. In effect, journalists argued that our angle of vision contained an alternative "image" of the Mezzogiorno with respect to what prevailed in public opinion[16] (while the cultural difficulties in the regularization of informal work that we had analyzed [Meldolesi, Arbitrio, Del Monaco 1996] represented — Barbara Fiammeri wrote in *Sole 24 Ore* — "a resounding anthropological thesis"). The campaign grew, overflowing a bit everywhere — from local newspapers to radio and television — producing echos in an interview that appeared in *Affari e Finanza*[17] and provoking a series of reactions, both for and against, which resulted in a whirlwind of meetings.

8 – What can be said about this briefly evoked episode? It can be observed in the first place that we were sitting on a volcano without knowing it, or rather without having the faintest idea that we might set it off. Yet ignite it did, and crackled on for several weeks. Viewed in retrospect, the traditional pessimistic image of an eternally backward and begging Mezzogiorno today looks worn out and tarnished. Constructed to emphasize the Southern emergency and to spur action, the image has over time become the umbrella of welfarism, finally (and inadvertently) spilling into the anti-Southern camp — it is this image of the South that sustains secessionism.

---

[16] In mid-April, on the sidelines of a conference on the Mezzogiorno, it was Giorgio Lonardi of *La Repubblica* and Antonello Talamanca of *Il Mondo* who suggested to me that this was indeed a general alternative. In particular I recall Talamanca's reaction to my explanations: "But Professor, this is not the image the country has of the South!"

[17] Actually a "collage" constructed with great skill by Alessandra Carini while "sifting through" some of my manuscripts.

It makes sense, then, that a section of the press and public welcomed with relief a less distressing prospect for the Mezzogiorno and the country. Faced with the widespread belief that the South is inhabited essentially by the unemployed, bureaucrats, pensioners and *Camorristi*, the media, for once, showed that there is in the Mezzogiorno a myriad of small businesses alongside medium and larger ones, and that Southerners are in the great majority a population of worker ants who get up early in the morning to go to their jobs. From one end of the country to the other, signs of relief and sympathy for this highly encouraging message flooded in .[18] And it was supported by a wealth of concrete examples—clothing, footwear, swimwear, linens, leather goods, jewelry, etc.—that created the momentum essential to the campaign. The country was more open to the new than they had imagined.

But change occurs along winding paths and is never black or white. While it was important to document an image other than the traditional one, it was not simply a case of one supplanting the other. Rather, a new condition came about in which a way of thinking was still prevalent, but it no longer had its traditional cogency, while at the same time, the issue of

---

[18] Aside from people from the North and the South who recognized themselves in the new perspective based on their own experience, I was especially surprised by the reaction of economists, sociologists, demographers, etc. I met casually who told me, "[N]ow I understand why there is no longer any emigration," or "why the South is not bursting," etc. Evidently, for these intellectuals the traditional image of an eternally ongoing and aggravated Southern emergency was not credible—they felt encouraged to finally articulate their disbelief. This brings up a delicate point. The intellectual grip of the traditional pessimistic view on people's minds was so tight that many did not find the courage to own up to how things were. They felt that this would undermine the "rationale" of the Mezzogiorno. This explains, psychologically, the drifting of an important part of Meridionalism—but it should certainly not condition our work. In the first place because the image we present is truthful, and the group of journalists, to their credit, testified to it before the country. Secondly because, as readers will see for themselves later, we intend to vigorously support the emergence of undocumented labor and the strengthening of Southern light industrialization.

small businesses and undeclared work now assumed an important function. Certainly, in the microcosm of those who engage professionally with the Mezzogiorno (one against the other – and armed!) there has been a competition to exploit the situation that has arisen *pro domo propria*.[19] But despite some angry reactions (with consequences such as those reported at the start of the chapter), the ancient regime was not restored. The way is now open to create a new consciousness.

9 – The issue can be looked at from a more a more general perspective. Thoroughly immersed as we are in our own specific situation, we struggle to see it as part of a larger developmental pattern. Thus, it was only *post factum*, and after banging my head against the problem,[20] that I began to see the changing image of the South from an international perspective.

For a less developed area or country – Albert Hirschman explains (1995, p. 191) – there are two mutually contradictory ways of pleading the cause of its own development to the outside world. One is to emphasize the dramatic nature of its condition so as to solicit public financing, and the other is to emphasize opportunities for private investment. The first of these, which in Latin America has taken the form of the "pessimistic view that mobilizes action," has prevailed for an entire historical era, supported by the reality of the Cold War and the progressive rhetoric of looming disaster, according to which if the country is not helped, it might slip into the opposing camp.

Undoubtedly, the Mezzogiorno has also with time developed a pessimistic outlook that has created more demoralization than

---

[19] Some thought that my work justified their own specific viewpoint. Many others – as mentioned above – on the basis of improvised documentation (and "hidden motives") were afraid that accepting the new approach would mean leaving the South to "fend for itself." Still others sensed a looming danger to their own vested interests.
[20] I am referring to chapters 2, 16 and 17 of Albert Hirschman's *A Propensity to Self-Subversion* (1995), which I recently reread in order to finalize the Italian edition.

action, a vision that throughout the declining phase of the First Republic fueled corporatism, clientelism and crime based on "communism at the gates" blackmail. From this point of view, the break with a vision that has by now become counterproductive seems almost a duty, which the particular political moment the country has gone through has brought into the light. This is not to say, however, that the Mezzogiorno can move expeditiously toward attracting investment from private sources. First, despite the good results from some large companies, the lessons of past experience are too bitter to allow hope for a quick turnaround. Moreover, as I will explain more fully below, important battles must be won to prepare the ground for such investments, including those involving domestic medium-sized enterprises that could considerably strengthen the propensity for light industrialization. Finally, it is perhaps possible to make a virtue of necessity — that is, to graft onto the necessary civil and institutional reorganization elements of support for Southern productive capacities that would enable the Mezzogiorno to gradually acquire a role as a true protagonist.

In conclusion, then, the event evoked above and the reflections it has provoked bring us new responsibilities that cannot be those of simply reversing the front. In a context of liberalization and of participation in the great European and international markets we must find the thread of a policy capable of taking on the many dualities of the southern condition.

10 – So let us return to the snapshot taken at the beginning – the "*tale e quale*," the spitting image, as they appropriately say in Neapolitan dialect. On the one hand we have a semi-legal society rooted in the family hearth, and on the other a propensity for light industrialization that made its mark in disguise and has now attracted attention. To transform this image of the

Mezzogiorno into proposals for action we need to schematize some aspects of it.

(a) The South is neither incomprehensible nor unchangeable. To comprehend it we need to explore it. A very simple approach is to penetrate into the productive and social life of small towns — where everyone knows everything about everybody — with the help of the local students and their families. The very clear dualities that emerge from these reconnaissances — between legality and illegality, inside and outside, private and public, producers and profit-makers, etc. — are the "handles" that possible change must grab on to, so to speak.

(b) In this regard, careful observation reveals that many of the ingredients or prerequisites of development that are said to be lacking in the Mezzogiorno — such as trust, civic-mindedness, a sense of the state, etc. — are not entirely absent. In any Southern town it is easy to detect elements of cooperation, collective identity and political participation. The truth is rather that the deficiencies easily found on these levels are related to a pessimistic and implosive tendency that makes Southerners feel inadequate with respect to their life aspirations.

This gives rise to a society that is at the same time both aggregated by family groups and peculiarly fragmented and distressed. The sense of powerlessness robs subjects of the ability to master their surroundings and leads them to develop propensities that express their need to escape from the reality oppressing them, but which they do not feel they need to explore further.[21] In addition, the sense of not being able to do what

---

[21] These impressions were verified through the very simple system of getting invited to my students' homes. It turned out that in general they underestimate the productive world around them. There are those who think of their town as an underdeveloped area, whereas later it turns out that it is home to some large factories. Some look at the small factories with a certain condescension, while others have not even noticed that they are humming along only a few kilometers away. There are those who prefer to gloss over illegal work because "in the village they don't talk about it"; some

should be done actually leads individuals to focus even more on "their own business," inadvertently reducing their energy even further. Misunderstanding of one's own situation turns into misunderstanding of oneself and the endemic tendency toward personal *depression*, experienced as a trap.

(c) However, while this implosive process propels the stagnation of collective life, poorly mobilized energy can suddenly find itself invigorated. It is precisely the subjects' having gotten used to a "low volume" life that leads to a surprising experience — the discovery that they have capacities and strengths of character that they thought they lacked. They set in motion a process that, through a "dissonant" experience, ends up modifying their own ideas. There follows a reevaluation of work, commitment, punctuality, initiative, saving, and entrepreneurial risk. This — in broad strokes — is the story of the small entrepreneurs who were the protagonists of the industrial successes mentioned above and of those whom they effectively involved.[22]

---

are obsessed with the Camorra, etc. Along with this lack of knowledge of how things actually are, one can observe the emergence of specific mental blind spots and an infatuation with cultural and political issues that go beyond the context. But there is an opposite tendency as well: there are students who know a lot about the place, things that many others can also "unearth" once such knowledge is appreciated. Finally, it is worth adding that once the implosive drive is identified, the careful observer easily finds it everywhere. It is typical, for example, that young people know what's going on in their town, but not in the town next door which may be part of the same production system. Moreover, in the South more than elsewhere, collective life is concentrated in the main arteries, while everything else, especially in the winter months, happens at low pressure, in a condition of perpetual waiting — a kind of quotidian vegetative state that does not help to shake off the sense of impotence that is perceived in the air and that one would like to dispel.

[22] In essence, the subjects do not realize that they are, one might say, like spools that are unwound or wound up and that it pays to live "wound up." As shown in the theses by Diego Rossano and Paola Alfano (who are now "in the home stretch") this is also true for public administration. Indeed, in a generally uninviting landscape, it is possible to encounter examples where latent energies have been vigorously mobilized. The cases studied by the two students of an assistance committee

For a Reasonable Economic Policy
11 – I shall therefore revisit the question from *Mezzogiorno, con Gioia*: What economic policy does a society such as the Mezzogiorno need? A policy—I answered (1992a, p. 82)—that is liberal and progressive. Liberal because the pessimistic and implosive spirit that pervades the South must be fought essentially through the market, freeing productive forces in their interaction with the market; and progressive because in order to meet that challenge, the South must be adequately supported. Such support must carefully avoid all forms of *quid pro quo* (and thus clientelism) and at the same time promote a massive assertion of state authority, starting with the fight against crime.[23] This is an approach that I argued for, in its economic aspects, in "A Framework for the South" (1996c).[24] I would now like to take it further.

In fact, with all due respect to Benedetto Croce, what is rational (unfortunately) is not necessarily real—so that we cannot expect our key to the problem to turn *ipso facto* into pure gold. Not that I doubt its wondrous virtues, of course. I merely observe that if we want to bring it to life, we must set it in the real world, where there exists a situation of interregnum, not to say confusion, about the policies to be followed. What is

---

of the municipality of Mugnano and of ten administrative innovation projects reported by the Civil Service Department acquire, from this point of view, paradigmatic significance. Their continuation over time shows that in Southern society there is a strong moral compensation (in personal and collective recognition) for those who, against all odds, succeed in making things work. Moreover, the meticulous study of these experiences can teach us much about the objective and subjective conditions that enable them and give us an idea of how we should behave in other contexts as well.

[23] The great problem of restoring state authority in the South is unfortunately underestimated. To listen informally to some officials, the focus of state intelligence is on large-scale crime, while small crime is not worth the effort because the current guarantee laws make it easy to get out of jail. This widely held view actually betrays a quiet-life mentality that favors the everyday forces of lawlessness, including the deeply entrenched forces of small-town crime.

[24] See chapter 7 in this volume.

more, these "first ideas" are being composed at a snail's pace by the National Conference on Employment for which I have already written a brief memorandum (Meldolesi 1998b). [25] Thus, instead of resuming the argument in broad strokes, it is worth clarifying some of its specific issues — those concerning how to intervene *cum grano salis* in the South's many dualities to push a society that essentially hangs in the balance in the desired direction.

12 - The first step in this brief excursus is to ask whether a reasonable policy for the situation we have described can emerge from the current debate and the deadlines now approaching. First of all, there are important policy proposals — such as the establishment of five free zones — which meet the requirements mentioned above and which could be complemented by other measures, such as the partial restoration of the taxation of social security contributions, the lowering of the price of certain public services and an across-the-board credit subsidy. From here an effective development package might emerge for all types of enterprises (large, medium and small), calibrated for different areas, which could be "adjusted" at regular intervals.[26]

Then there are other measures that are automatic in nature (that is, which do not involve any discretion from the point of view of the administration), but they are not indirect like the previous ones — that is, they do not take place unseen, behind the recipient's back. At the same time, neither do they involve any kind of rationing — they are activated by a simple application that anyone could submit — so that if properly implemented (and I stress this *if*), they could achieve good results. Belonging to this group is the restoration for the Mezzogiorno

---

[25] See chapter 8 in this volume.
[26] My views on this are contained in 1990, 1992a, 1994a, and 1996c. On the matter of the abolition of the taxation of welfare payments, cf. Viesti 1996.

of the "Sabatini law" (which, by repaying a large part of the expenses actually incurred for investments in machinery, has in the past made a significant contributions to the formation of local systems in the Center-North) and the use of EU funds for job creation in the Mezzogiorno (which is already under way at 20-60 million per job), a measure that could encourage the legalization of irregular labor.[27]

On the other hand, it seems unlikely that near-term policy can effectively be based on these types of measures and on implementation subject to periodic monitoring and evaluation aimed at gradually increasing their performance. If this actually happened, we would already have come a long way in encouraging light industrialization.[28] But as things stand, this approach will undoubtedly have to coexist with others, such as the financing of new companies, the prioritizing of major works and infrastructure, an emphasis on agreements between social partners, etc.

13 – The latter has both a specific and a general character. Beyond ideological comparisons (concerning wages, for example—a comparison that seems to me unreasonable since the wages of "strong" irregular workers are not far from the minimum wages of regular workers) I would not expect in the short term to see much progress. The greater receptivity of unions has brought significant results, but only in the narrow sector of large

---

[27] More generally, I think the country should negotiate with the EU a transitional phase of redirection for Southern life during which a large part of EU funding for the Mezzogiorno would be channeled automatically and indirectly.

[28] In addition, the types of intervention mentioned in the text can be set alongside a logically inverse form based on high administration accountability and beneficiary involvement (Meldolesi 1996c). It is a useful formula for specific tasks, such as eliminating pockets of poverty or breaking the condition of subordination in this or that market through the formation of new enterprises (such as those in Law 44/1986).

and medium-sized enterprises. The agreement on training inside the factory and not outside is welcome, but it remains to be seen whether it will in any way affect the vast training sector where "disreputable" interests and behavior lurk. The policies on agreements for "re-entry" from illegal work have so far yielded little in the way of results.[29] On the other hand, to date no one seems willing to acknowledge a simple truth, namely that a major obstacle to the emergence from undeclared work lies in the danger that a worker who has been brought into compliance, will "slack off" because he or she feels ultra-guaranteed by existing laws and practices.

And as for the general level, it is well known that the policy of the government proceeds through agreement between the parties. It is hard to imagine that up through the branches of opposing organizations and the political system as a whole, the great welfarist push for a stable and secure position that we see so plainly will not be felt. The very high youth unemployment rate is indicative of a desire to leave behind the world of irregular employment. Even the stones of the Mezzogiorno know that the public or big company jobs for which there is such pressing demand are precisely the kind that the Southern economy does not spontaneously create.

More generally, it should not be believed that the fall of the big criminals and major clientelist politicians in the South

---

[29] Promising, however, is the agreement on lengthening the training period. It accommodates a current practice in the Murge "sofa triangle" (between Basilicata and Puglia) under which the young worker rotates among several firms by signing a training-work contract every two years. Another semi-regulatory system has made headway in Aversa on the sidelines of discussions about a local territorial agreement. In order to form a consortium and thus take advantage of the shared services provided by the pact, a good number of small footwear firms have declared themselves artisans with the idea of turning their surplus workers into subcontractors. Finally, in many parts of the South there is a practice of regularizing labor by simultaneously establishing specific agreements between the parties (regarding daily production, hours, duties, wages, etc.).

111

marked the collapse of Southern pathologies. In a condition of confusion, social pressures affect one side or the other of the collective conscience and hence there are oscillations. While it is true that on the whole the "Clean Hands" period meant a retreat of pathologies and a step forward for labor in the South, it is also true that in the past year a number of symptoms indicate a resumption of welfarist pressure — to use the current euphemism.

14 – Is it possible that this collective pressure is not having an impact? In short, no, it isn't. If nothing else, while the measures discussed above would "only" invigorate the Southern economy, money spent directly can be seen, and therefore people understand it at a glance in the South — it plays an important role in consensus building. Of course, this does not necessarily mean a return to the welfarist glories of the past. But we should expect that, having gone out the door, welfarist pressure will show its face at the window. This is already clear from the behavior of local governments. Unable to mobilize pre-existing resources blocked by free riding, they are looking for new domestic and international financing. And this is without mentioning the various attempts to break the public hiring freeze (most recently at the post office — as the saying goes, "the best post is always a post at the post office!" [o posto a posta è sempre o meglio posto!]

Now, at the Employment Conference it is already to be expected that large companies, Southern ones included, will seek, with the agreement of the unions, to make use of such pressure by proposing the creation of new factories with state money — the so-called program agreements (accordi di programma). In addition, they are likely to talk about targeted financing, new technology, major projects, etc., without making any real effort to understand the very unflattering record of past experiences of the same kind.

Even limiting ourselves to public works, in the first place it is well known that the South is littered with bloated high-waste projects, even in the most remote towns (while small municipalities in the North-Center have been neglected). Moreover, many finished works are not being used (or are being used for private purposes). Others are poorly managed, while still others are not yet finished or abandoned half finished. Shouldn't small measures first be taken to raise the often very low return on investments already made? Of course, I realize that because of its weight in the southern economy, the recovery of the building sector is an important priority. It can indeed be facilitated by the launch of some major infrastructure projects, and there are guarantees for their construction today that we did not have in the past. But the country needs transparency and wise use of investments, both new and old.

One would have to be blind not to see that much of the national and Southern opposition to the change in the image of the South mentioned above has come from the vast section that aspires to direct public funding and the welfarist/corporatist bloc that struggles to reintroduce itself in other guises.[30] Hence

---

[30] It is peculiar that one of the strengths of this setup is the claim that it does not take into consideration even the existence of the informal economy. As it is engaged in irregular practices it does not legally exist and therefore should not exist. Any reasoning about the Mezzogiorno should be limited to the legal sector.

The same of course goes for the statistics. It matters little that a vast underground world exists in the South and that therefore the workers, their products, and the enterprises themselves cannot be accurately surveyed (for the simple reason that in acting irregularly they have an interest in concealing their condition). But it does matter that the statistics say officially that there is a sea of unemployment in the South—that is, of people who aspire to legal employment. This rift between legal and illegal is so deeply embedded in mainstream consciousness that it has become an effective obstacle to understanding of the entire Southern situation.

the all-out defense of the unemployment rate, the real talking fetish of the Southern scene.[31]

15 – To help us understand this, let us recall the common perception that a desire for a stable and secure job is an offspring of the implosive pessimistic tendency mentioned above. Discontented with their own condition, as they often are, many families push their children up the educational ladder with the mirage of "a position." We need to understand what it means to them when their child enters the Guardia di Finanza, or their apprehension over the fantasy of graduation. Or how the passion for a position takes precedence even in the homes of self-employed workers and small business owners who are overburdened with work and feel socially discriminated against.

With the turn of the Republic and the passing of peak criminal business—mentioned previously—the prospects for light industrialization have improved. But it should not be assumed that definitive change is just around the corner. At the mass level there is a general opacity of awareness, a willingness created by the implosive tendency to think that "all the saints will be there for us"—just satisfy your own needs and somehow preserve social respectability. This is a trap that it is always easy to fall into.

---

[31] As they say in Rome, public money is a temptation for everyone. It is logical, then, that the circles just mentioned should welcome any reasoning that pushes the state to spend the money it takes in in one way or another...as long as it is the way into their pockets. One route long used is to dramatize the Southern situation starting with the unemployment rate (without respect to the actual facts or even the proportion or rather disproportion that exists between the enormous demand for jobs and the inevitably limited supply that would be produced by a policy intervention). But if the fetish of the unemployment rate is called into question? What justification would these Roman lobbying circles have? Nor can it comfort them that, with the prospect indicated above of the emergence into the light of irregular labor, the Mezzogiorno would gain a far greater number of regular workers.

It is imperative, then, as we now know, to vigorously limit the creation of "positions" and thereby prevent discretionary rationing (you yes, you no) from rekindling the spiral of clientelism and free-riding, behind which the specter of the country's bankruptcy has been lurking for some time now. But we must also have the courage to state that in order to channel national and community resources for productive purposes in an automatic and indirect (or direct but not rationed) manner according to the guidelines mentioned above, and to gradually clear the way for industrial expansion and the attraction of capital from outside, it is essential to *dislodge free-riding* wherever it is found, send the idlers packing, reduce the privileges of non-performers, and recover the efficiency of the entire public system in enforced stages. In addition, it is necessary to gradually reduce the tax burden on the citizens, especially those who are struggling with it—a reduction that must be accompanied by a contraction in spending, and which can be partly offset by regularization of work and a consequent broadening of the taxpayer base.

Only in this way—that is, by prodding citizens to face the market without comfortable alternatives, progressively legalizing the associated way of life so as to gradually dislodge implosive pessimism and the propensity for stealth, and boosting their confidence in their own abilities by elevating individual and collective contributions—only in this way is it possible to envision an authentic restoration of the Southern condition that will have beneficial consequences for the entire country.

In Conclusion

16 – We have thus identified several ways of evaluating different economic policies and the concrete means, almost palpable I would say, of disentangling them. These show us that there is a dividing line in the Mezzogiorno that we must not lose

sight of between proposals and behaviors that are compatible with the development of the market economy and democracy, and proposals and behaviors that are anything but. Of course, in the interregnum that has now been created in the South we cannot expect these latter to disappear with a wave of a magic wand. It is imperative to find temporary balances and intelligent solutions by which to navigate the rocky shoals. But the course must be clear and must yield tangible results at regular intervals.

On the other hand, if we finally plunge into a local reality with this line of reasoning in mind, we face the typical dilemma of the politics of underdevelopment — a condition that to paraphrase Keynes might be called an underemployment equilibrium of human energy. On the one hand, it is not difficult to say what should be done — we are if anything spoiled for choice. On the other, it is far from easy to achieve even a small part of what should be done.

To exemplify, I recall that for a time light industrialization went hand in hand with the breakdown of municipal governments.[32] Inevitably, one of the first goals of the new administrations was to get citizens to pay their taxes, starting with the taxes on water and garbage — a task undeniably far from easy. Then it was a matter of "better spending" of the taxpayer's money — also not an easy task, because a large part of the budget ends up in the salaries of employees who often have second jobs and feel completely protected by the law (if not by

---

[32] We are used to thinking that economics and politics go together, for better or worse. But in our story, this is not the case. In Grumo Nevano, taxes for essential services were not being paid even by the staff responsible for collecting them. And after three years of effort to restart the machine and citizens complaining about having to start paying taxes — the mayor wonders if it would not have been better to declare the municipality bankrupt! When I asked a businessman the reason for all this, he answered that he had given all his attention to production. Clearly the hypothesis that it is possible in the South to engineer a reasonable path of economic and political advancement is a gamble indeed.

the crime syndicate itself). Again, we need to clamp down on the business-criminal mentality that has long dominated local government and is responsible for the widespread speculative fever visible even to the naked eye.

In essence, on every issue of normal administration the path immediately becomes bumpy. This is not to underestimate the great endeavors undertaken by many new administrations with the direct election of the mayor. Neither does it mean underestimating the significance that some of these instruments may have—such as the 44/'86 companies,[33] the development missions (Missioni di sviluppo), or the territorial pacts (Patti territoriali) that bring social and institutional productive forces together for the first time on the great issue of local development. Rather, we need to emphasize the great hardship of emergence into legality, i.e., of productive forces throwing off the camouflage—economic, social and legal.[34] While society

---

[33] Recently (1996, p. 15) Giacomo Becattini forcefully denounced "the equivocal nature of any policy for small businesses as such." "It is not," he observed, "a matter of the generic promotion of small business start-ups, destined for the most part for a rapid end, but to promote their emergence in socio-cultural and institutional contexts and commodity areas where they have some chance of surviving and thriving." I do not know whether in writing these remarks Becattini had in mind the case of Imprenditorialità Giovanile (IG) [Youth Entrepreneurship], which is undoubtedly our country's premier small business creation experience, or whether he was affected by the usual obfuscation of Southern affairs that afflicts so many Italian intellectuals. I only know that in so writing he has implicitly raised a problem. The enterprises created by the IG in a decade number about a thousand and their survival rate is high (80%). The reason for their creation was probably the prevailing public perception that in the South there are no industrial activities. But their survival probably indicates the reverse—that they were to a large extent part of an incipient process of Southern light industrialization.

[34] To understand the complexity of the issue, it is worth listening to the many voices of artisans, self-employed workers and small entrepreneurs who denounce the imbalance that exists between their condition and ultra-guaranteed public employment. "I feel like someone who has a stall in the middle of the street (selling contraband cigarettes)," said a small businessman to Liliana Bàculo, clearly feeling the weight of the semi-legal status he finds himself in. Symptoms of a propensity to emerge now seem to be on the rise after a period of strong submersion that followed the 1992-3 crisis—think, for example, of the formation of the association

today basically runs on an undercurrent, outwardly showing its thin legal facade while concealing its many irregular aspects, a series of stirrings suggest that such a situation could be legalized and that this could happen along a trajectory of industrial success. If nothing else, there is no doubt that the hive of small businesses has come to life in spite of all the Southern pathologies. This is a sign of a capacity for self-sufficiency (in coping with difficulties) at the highest level, a sign of considerable internal strength—of personal conviction, family cohesion, and possibly even the "strength of desperation," the sign of a collective subsoil of capability, cooperation and common historical origin—of a mass cultural richness that has indeed not been lost. What energies might be released by these deep-rooted assets if the surrounding environment became more "friendly" to industrial production?

17 – Like all wagers, ours too is highly uncertain. It takes us along a narrow path between overhanging cliffs. External support for the Southern economy may be insufficient and may push it toward submergence or dissolution, or it may be more substantial but deviated in the direction of free-riding and psychological displacement. And in addition, general policy has to accord with that of the social partners and with local policy. Once one part of the issue is settled, the weight of change—if change is what we are after—falls on the others. While national policy and that of the social partners are moving towards clarification, local administrations—especially at the regional level—are known to be experiencing notable and genuinely worrying difficulties.

---

of young entrepreneurs of S. Giuseppe Vesuviano. But it is difficult to say how much this is a consequence of an underlying trend and how much is related to expectations fueled by the launch of the Prodi government.

Can we be sure we have fitted the main pieces of the mosaic into their proper places? We have spoken of the decline of the "pessimistic view that mobilizes action" and the opening of a glimmer of understanding of the Mezzogiorno. But we have said nothing about a possible alternative that might recharge the batteries of Southern democratic political engagement. And yet even in this area some things have moved in the past year. Franco Cassano's book, *Il Pensiero Meridiano* (Southern Thought [1996]), the return of interest in the works of Albert Camus, and the Manifesto on Southern thinking by a group of intellectuals are evidence of the search for a viewpoint rooted in the culture of the Mediterranean, in the encounter between land and sea in this ancient waterhole of humanity. It is a view of differences, democracy and federalism that fortunately is encouraging and reasonably optimistic about the prospects for the Mezzogiorno.

In the fragmented condition of Southern life, this new trend has sprung from humanistic culture and the social sciences. Its position against imported modernism has so far kept it danger-ously distant from the reality of production. But if it grasps the great opportunity that exists at the productive level to make use of the skills and heritage of a thousand-year-old culture, it will be able to play a significant role in correcting adverse spontane-ous trends and in promoting a full-blown Southern flowering.

6. FROM A POSITION TO A JOB[*]

1 – Concerning the problem of employment, a traditional way of thinking often resurfaces in current publications, which says "less work, but work for everyone." Of course, I do not deny that there may be specific conditions, like the Volkswagen case, for example, where it makes sense to find an internal labor-sharing arrangement that allows a surplus workforce to remain on the job, perhaps pending a recovery in demand. Nor do I deny that certain particularly ungrateful sectors may require further reductions in working time. It seems to me, however, that under today's conditions, using the old slogan as a generalized banner is somewhat anachronistic.

It is a buzzword of the boom years. Its meaning softened the harsh rejection of Fordist labor, but the viewpoint was the same. It meant that assembly-line work and related jobs had to be spread over more people. At the same time, the slogan appealed to those in need of work. To put it in the Tuscan manner, it was a way of "killing two birds with one stone..."

"Less work, but work for everyone" was a watchword of the challenge to the scientific organization of labor in its declining stage. The work it refers to is the passive and repeated work of Taylorism/Fordism. But in the twenty years since, this sort of work has declined sharply. What sense does it make to reintroduce the slogan today, since largely it has lost its main redistributive message? Presumably, its intention is to claim a fixed job from whoever is in charge (industry, the state). It is

[*] From: Meldolesi,L. (2021), *Mezzogiorno con gioia*, pp. 197-203. This is a revised version of an essay originally written at the request of *Il progetto*, the magazine of Cisl. I decided to write in a straightforward way, without pretense. "It will not be published" —I thought. But it appeared in No. 12, 1996 of that magazine. Moreover, the leaders of Cisl-Cesos asked me, together with Luigi Frey, to open their International Conference in Rome (spring 1997).

precisely this claim, made at a delicate moment in our national life, that prompts me to write in response.

2 – The decline of Fordism leaves behind a complex intellectual legacy. Keynesian macroeconomics is thoroughly steeped in that historical era, labor appearing as a mere quantity that may or may not be enlisted by capital on the basis of existing techniques. Its leadership, its spirit of initiative, is generally absent. But agency of this sort is actually the main feature of the industrial revolution in which we find ourselves. Instead of passive, scientifically predetermined work, today it is active work that pays — skilled, collaborative, "awake" work, which actually utilizes for productive purposes a significant part of an individual's manifold potentialities. It is work (self-employed and salaried) that often produces a fusion of goods and services with inputs from both, uses the relationship between production and consumption in a symbiotic way, and functions through local systems and globalizing networks and so on.

In short, an entire Fordist world has fallen into crisis. Yet, at the same time, it continues to condition our minds. No wonder this causes dismay, even in those who have lived somewhat reflexively through the glories and misfortunes of its trajectory. "There is no work, not anymore," is what they say in the South, referring precisely to the secure job promised by the Fordist era.

It is a disturbing thought, undermining the plans of countless middle-class families and others from modest backgrounds who put their children through school to ensure their future. "And what if our efforts were in vain?" — is what shows on the dismayed faces of so many parents. It is a question that leads many to the same unison response. We need to "offer secure jobs."

3 – But then if we look at things closely, we realize that the reality is more complex. Fordism did not do well in the South, to the point that for an entire era Southern workers were considered to be a working class in training, their impatience with the Fordist yoke underlies a series of public and private failures. How then do we explain the current nostalgia for that time? The truth is that the object of Southern yearning has never been Fordist labor, but rather a stable position. It is what I affectionately call the "Pulcinella syndrome" – that pressing need to pull oneself out of the precariousness of a weak labor market, the irrepressible (and understandable) desire to consume like those in the North – to find, that is, this blessed stable and secure position, whatever it may be. Indeed, taking it for granted that the work will not be exciting.

Not least in this attitude is a subtle vein of embarrassment from which two consequences follow. Often, having once got the position, the person loses interest in the job and thinks of other things (a second job, personal matters, etc.). Secondly, the aura of social standing that surrounds the person who has obtained the position does not correspond to his or her inner convictions. The "settled" individual suffers from a lack of job satisfaction and at heart has little self-esteem. This causes a visible sinking tendency. In industrial Fordism there was still the need to sweat and the possibility of blaming someone, but in public para-Fordism this does not exist. Envied and despised, unsure of themselves but unable to give up their privilege, those who now feel "okay" tend to isolate themselves in idleness.

4 – Here we encounter a problem typical of the Southern condition. Onto an ancient culture that lends itself to a thousand kinds of dodges, the habitual "propensity for cunning" spontaneously grafts a kind of defensive language that casually changes the cards on the table.

Often, "effort" ["fatica" in Neapolitan] and "position" do not coincide. To make such a separation, the subject plays the game on two tables—legal-union culture and the reality of the South. The former represents the world of aspiration, of the constitutional right to work, and of the abstract "worker"; the latter, the prosaic daily condition of work that, *faute de mieux*, one is forced to accept. Observe, for example, the following conversation. "Excuse me, are you unemployed?" "Of course." The interlocutor pretends to misunderstand, "Jesus, Jesus, and how many are you in the family?" "Four" "And the others don't work?" "No, only I go out to work."

As we can see, from a semiological point of view, the reasoning of the unemployed person represents an updated version of the traditional need of the working classes to "get" something from the current powerholder (the lord, the foreigner, the state, the North). As such, it stems from a relationship of asymmetry and subordination, but it poses a danger, because it ends up perpetuating, and even aggravating, that very condition. Indeed, exactly contrary to what economics preaches, here the pursuit of individual interest has a disastrous effect on collective interest.

The same can be said for the issue of unemployment. Here again one senses in the current reasoning "a collusive game, as perfect as it is perverse, being played with official scientific data."[1] I am of course referring to the so-called unemployment drama. This is a general alarm sounded by the mass media every time data is published on this topic.

It is now known (and easily verifiable) that such data are literally crammed with young people chasing stable jobs. But in any case—their publication represents a magical opportunity to bring together the aforementioned concerns and to turn them

---

[1] Nicolaus (1997).

into a lobbying force. In this way, a double effect occurs. On one hand, growth in the youth unemployment rate in reality expresses the increase in the level of social pressure for positions; on the other hand, its publication further fuels such pressure.

This youth unemployment rate has increased rapidly to 65%. This is an average and includes areas in the interior where the rate is much lower. The conclusion therefore is that in the "flesh" of the South (in the plains) more or less all the young people consider themselves unemployed — precisely because they are holding out for their position. It is a dangerous game because the serious situation of undeclared work in the South and the fact that much of it is underpaid can transform the illusions of the unemployed subspecies of young people into real drama (a sort of self-fulfilling prophecy).

5 – I think that on the contrary it is in the country's every interest to distinguish between the different phenomena and effectively handle them.

The unreasonable data on unemployment are one thing; the huge reality of undeclared work is another. And a third, more serious still, is poverty. Instead of dealing with these last two phenomena, as any civilized country would, attention is at regular intervals focused on the unemployment rate. This rate is undoubtedly a product of young high school graduates' desire for employment, but it also comes from the poverty of the culture, the lack of clarity of political and trade union forces, and the asymmetrical process of North-South interaction mentioned above.

In the Motherland of law, legality (in theory) sets the law, while semi-legal areas attract little attention because they are lackluster and because ... in principle they should not exist. Thus, it happens that the legal-union norms established in collective Northern practice and sanctioned by Parliament apply in the South only to a certain portion (more public than private) of labor activity. Elsewhere one enters a kind of no man's land where, however, an often-vibrant potential is concentrated to-day—capacities and resources that could profoundly change the economic and social reality of our country.

6 – Here we finally come to the point. The prevailing public image of an eternally depressed South, populated by pensioners, lazy people and criminals is, fortunately for us, not true. In recent years, as the welfare system entered a crisis and dragged part of the productive apparatus along with it, the stratospheric percentage of government spending on Southern income (over 70 percent) finally began to decline, and light industrialization began not only to emerge into view, but to flourish. The visible growth in locally produced goods and services along with the resurgence of tourism brought to the forefront another Mezzogiorno which has only recently begun to make headlines.

Today we know that this is a very broad phenomenon affecting (in "bone" and "flesh") all regions of the South. It is family-based, straddling the formal and informal sectors, and has a pronounced preference for the "cluster" and the district. It is gradually forming self-sustaining labor markets despite still-significant market weakness, an effect of the IT revolution and participation in the national and international market. It mainly manufactures "Made in Italy" products, both on its own and on behalf of third parties, and it is at the heart of the recent leap forward of Southern exports.

Understandably, in a society as fragmented, sedentary and hungry as the South, this vigorous spread of small business, often underground, has so far not attracted the attention of the professional middle classes in the city centers. This is without doubt a gap to be bridged and an adjustment to be facilitated, especially for institutions and associations along with political and trade-union circles. At bottom, I seem to glimpse a general problem of comprehension of the process underway and the consequent choices. There exists in the Mezzogiorno a strong pathological current that unfortunately conditions many circles of society. With the decline of Fordism and the public apparatus, this current, though put to the test by the events of recent years, seems to be seeking new fields of operation. Against it, small-scale industrialization has spread but is nevertheless kept at bay by official society and even forced to resort to camouflage. Shouldn't the trade unions welcome this resurgent prominence of labor (self-employed and dependent) by supporting the process of change?

A DIFFERENT MERIDIONALISM

7. A FRAMEWORK FOR THE SOUTH[*]

1. Alain Peyrefitte (1998) has published a new edition of his lectures at the Collége de France on "miracles" in economics — a topic, the dust jacket explains, that has been at the center of his thinking for forty years. This small volume of "comparative development ethology" revolves around a general thesis that is worth mentioning.

The natural-historical condition of humanity, argues Peyrefitte, is not a condition of development but rather of its absence (*non-développement*). Instead of asking why so many people have lived or live in poverty, it is more logical to ask the reverse question — to try to understand the miracle of development.

Examining a series of cases, both ancient (Hebrews, Greeks, Phoenicians) and modern (Dutch, British, American), the author argues, leads to the conclusion that to explain miracles in economics, a "third intangible factor" alongside capital and labor must be considered, one that is difficult to grasp — namely, the "ethic of competitive trust." This is the unleashing of the human moral potential that lies in all of us trusting both one another and our common future. It is a factor that little by little assumes the most diverse forms and indelibly characterizes the life of a people. It is an aspect of freedom on which our adventure fundamentally depends.

This authoritative thesis, supported by the vast contemporary literature on the importance of trust, social capital and culture for economic development, suggests we focus our attention (from both an interpretive and normative viewpoint) on the relationship between economic and non-economic factors — where the latter can be positive or negative, spontaneously generated, or the effect of conscious policies. This is precisely what I have been trying to understand with regard to the

[*] From Meldolesi, L. (2021c), *Mezzogiorno con gioia!* Pp. 81-106. This essay from the spring of 1994 was originally published in No. 90 of *Economia e politica industriale* [Economics and Industrial Policy] (Meldolesi 1996c). The revised (and abridged) version reproduced here appeared, as ch. 2, in Meldolesi (2001).

Mezzogiorno, moving in the intellectual wake of Albert Hirschman.

Logical Structure

2. In fact, at the heart of chapter 2 of this volume, "Mezzogiorno, with Joy" is the problem of strengthening motivations and behaviors (whether of peasant, artisan or "cultured" origin) that are favorable to development and combating the negative ones (which I later called the "three scourges"[1]), either directly or through the indirect effect of economic forces.

In "complicating economics," my focus was thus on the non-economic aspects of the Southern equation. But this did not mean underestimating the economic ones. In particular, with respect to the assumptions of the "Optimal Monetary Area," I emphasized automatic rebalancing, occurring indirectly, as the tool that is most independent of social conditioning (whether clientelist or from politics/labor unions). Now I would like to clarify that according to my reasoning, respect for economic "fundamentals" is a routine matter.

Indeed, historical experience shows that development in a given territory is powerfully driven by favorable differentials in labor costs with respect to productivity. This was the case of the Southern US, and is true today of Northern Mexico, as well as of small European countries such as Ireland and Portugal grappling with the EU's market and currency, and of the northern Italian regions that benefit from a relatively advantageous location compared to Switzerland, Austria, or southern Germany. It is a key aspect of the question, and illustrates conversely the structural handicap that besets the Mezzogiorno, aggravated (in addition) by distance from markets, environmental risk, cultural and bureaucratic problems, issues of public order, etc. The goal, therefore, is to "climb the slope," — out of the condition of relative minority status in which Southern life objectively unfolds.

---

[1] Originally in Meldolesi 1998a, ch. 2. Now translated in Stame, N., ed. (2024), the first volume in this trilogy of "Our Mezzogiorno."

3. I should first of all mention that the following pages were originally written as a reaction to the misunderstanding that initially surrounded the economic policy theses I proposed in "Mezzogiorno, with Joy." This prompted me to seek a more condensed formulation.[2] The point of departure was the observation of a southern society that has its own productive life (based mostly on small businesses), but which is turned in upon itself, clinging to types of behavior that only partly correspond to the democratic market economy system we intend to build. This led to the idea of acting simultaneously on two levels. On the one hand, pushing the Mezzogiorno even more into a confrontation with the market so that it gradually corrects its pathologies (through cognitive dissonance, meta-preferences, self-reflections and redirections) and increasingly gets capacities and resources mobilized and moving in the desired direction. And on the other, vigorously supporting entrepreneurs through public assistance, so that their businesses are actually successful in their impact with the market.

---

[2] The 1994 version of this text began as follows: "It is reported that one fine day Dante Alighieri heard a craftsman mercilessly mispronouncing some verses of the Divine Comedy. Indignant, he took some tools from the latter's workshop and threw them into the middle of the street. "What are you doing," cried the artisan, "are you crazy?" "Not at all," replied Alighieri, "I am doing what you did to me." Of course, any parallel with the great poet can only be part of some Homeric fabrication. But the very fact that this little story came back to me while I was searching for the roots of this "Framework for the South" suggests that it too is the result (constructive,I hope) of a rebellious impulse. In fact, faced with the anticipated shipwreck—which then punctually occurred—represented by the Intervento Straordinario for the Mezzogiorno, I found shelter in a number of propitious concepts, such as the automatic and indirect character of generalized intervention, the accountability for results of the officials in charge of specific measures, the progressive involvement of the beneficiaries, and ongoing iterative evaluation (providing an in-depth assessment of what has been done which then becomes essential for shaping new interventions). When I realized that this long-pursued perspective was being passed over in silence, obfuscated or misunderstood, I decided to look for a new version of it. It thus happened that early in the morning on an empty, slow-moving train bound for Naples the framework I am now proposing began to take shape under the amused eyes of Nicoletta Stame."

The systematization of this viewpoint, which simultaneously advocates liberalization and intervention, paved the way for the meeting with the "Artimino group."

Indeed, in the face of the crisis that had struck the Mezzogiorno, the beauty of this framework lay first and foremost in its demonstration that it was possible to escape the distressing choice of either further reducing support for the South with the certainty of exacerbating the crisis or maintaining it with the risk of further fueling welfarism. To the economist struggling with these alternatives, the essay showed a way out. With a strictly anti-welfare approach, it was possible to usefully reformulate support for the South — through measures that were both general (of an automatic and indirect nature) and specific (implying administration responsibility and beneficiary involvement).

4. On the other hand, it should be kept in mind that the path of my work is by no means linear. Whenever I encounter a line of research, I feel the need to develop it, leading the initial observation to its consequences. I seek to unravel, you might say, the little miniature world it contains. But then a second phase takes over — placing the results in a more complex historical-logical framework [...].[3]

There is in the South, I originally wrote, a widely extended nebula, entrenched and ever-present, of small businesses desperately trying to circumvent a thicket of legitimate and illegitimate fiscal, administrative, payroll, union and criminal constraints. Living in a rather hostile environment for their businesses and often worried about making ends meet, many traders opt, typically, for a low-profile image, if not for outright camouflage. It is a kind of widespread modesty that in small towns in the South perversely credits the primacy of the educated — of public careers, the lawyer, the notary.

---

[3] Which indeed happened later (Meldolesi, 2001) and may (and perhaps should) happen in the future.

Of course, it is true—according to a Braudelian conceptualization[4]—that in the South, the upper echelon is very slim compared to the European average. And it is also true that the level of the market is relatively "underweight." But in certain areas small and medium-sized firms are numerous. And they are complemented by many tiny ventures—an everyday reality that tapers off in jumps (like the terraces of the Amalfi coast) down to the myriad forms of *carpe diem*.

How to strengthen this vast fabric? How to reduce the too abundant "storms" that besieges it? How to increase its role in collective life in order to foster broader rehabilitation?

5. "Mezzogiorno, with Joy," as mentioned above, asserts the need for a liberal and progressive economic policy—to further impel actors into the market (the true antidote to "welfarism") and at the same time support them in their impact with it. The text thus deals with the psychological return on government spending—that is, the positive or negative consequences that it can produce for the behavior of the beneficiaries.[5] Alongside the behavior-inducing or non-inducing effect of spending on the economy (in terms of connections, investment, consumption, etc.) it questions the following polarity: Public spending, by placing under- or non-utilized capacities in motion, can induce "virtuous" behaviors and outcomes, but it can also push beneficiaries (and the economic structure itself) toward unedifying shores.

Strengthening the positive effects and reducing the negative ones as much as possible then becomes the primary purpose of a true development strategy. It is an approach that can be schematized (and then commented on) as follows: In order to account for the clientelist "temptation" of the system, it is best to indicate the effects (economic and behavioral) separately with

---

[4] Braudel (1980) and Braudel (1981); Meldolesi (1984).

[5] Later, while I was writing Ch. 5 of *Spender meglio* (1992a), Nicoletta Stame showed me some illuminating pages from Ignazio Silone (1968, pp. 165-177). Unfortunately, Silone's voice was not picked up at all by Meridionalism—neither that of the government nor of the opposition.

respect to the administration and the beneficiaries. In addition, this decoupling should be repeated to isolate the behaviors versus the economic effects expected from each measure, so as to obtain eight combinations. This allows attention to be focused on the two polarities that lie at the respective extremes of an ideal spectrum of possible interventions and which, for reasons we will touch on below, are (relatively) "impervious" to clientelist conditioning. One of these is defined by the automatism in the disbursement of benefits and the indirect form of their use, and the other is defined by the personal responsibility of officials and the involvement of the beneficiaries.

In our diagram (Fig. 1) such relationships exist alongside those that are behavior-inducing and permissive for the administration and the beneficiaries. We thus arrive at six independent and combinable dual criteria for logically ordering the interventions. We can combine them into three pairs depending firstly on whether the support granted is automatic or nonautomatic on the administration side and is received indirectly or directly on the beneficiary side (Box I); secondly, depending on whether or not the administration is responsible for the desired outcome (and evaluates it accordingly) and whether or not the intervention generates the progressive involvement of the beneficiary (Box II); and thirdly, depending on whether it follows a behavior-inducing (stimulating) or permissive rationale both on the decision-making side and on the utilization side (Box III). Following these criteria, we would argue that the characteristics: automatic, indirect, responsible (and evaluative), inclusive, and behavior-inducing produce in any case better consequences for behavior and the economy than their opposites (Fig. 1; legend).

An initial clarification
6. My contribution concerns the first two boxes of the diagram, while the third briefly alludes to the reasoning in Albert Hirschman's *The Strategy of Economic Development* (1958) — that is, to the "micro-technological" approach, according to which

it is best to privilege the kind of actions that (due to unbalanced growth, reversal of current relationships, multiple and robust connections, etc.) have an inducing, rather than simply permissive effect on development. They set in motion capacities and resources (especially managerial) that would otherwise remain hidden, scattered or badly utilized. In doing so, such interests end up acting indirectly on behavior through proven psychological mechanisms, pushing it in the direction of the market economy and democracy.

FIGURE 1

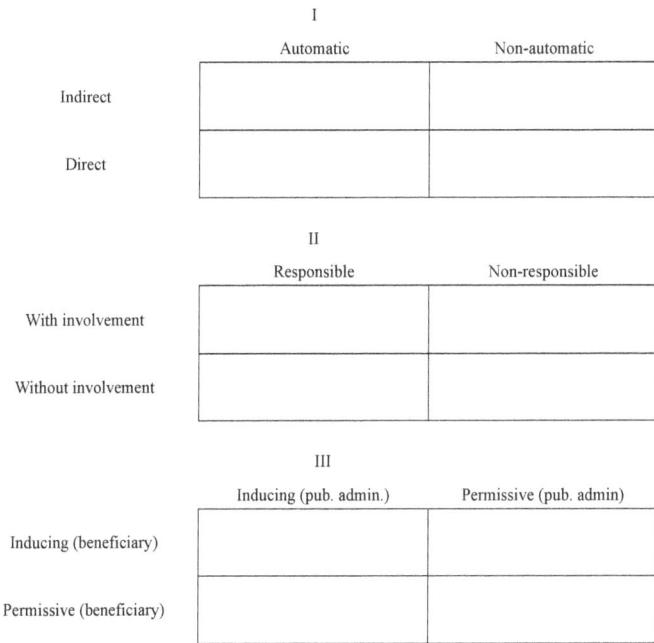

Automatic > Non-automatic

Indirect > Direct

Responsible (evaluating) > Non-responsible (not evaluating)

With involvement > Without involvement

Inducing (pub. admin.) > Permissive (pub. admin.)

Inducing (beneficiary) > Permissive (beneficiary)

FIGURE 2

	Responsible	Non-responsible
Direct		
Indirect		

Taking from "Mezzogiorno, with Joy" the need to examine the effects of government spending on behavior (along with those on the economy), I place here alongside the ultra-synthetic evocation of Hirschman's classic analysis an argument about the instruments of intervention, privileging, as will become clear later, those that are automatic and indirect and those that are empowering and involving, because in different ways they allow the dangers of clientelist brokering to be minimized.

In addition, the scheme can be supplemented by responsible action by the administration and direct action by the beneficiaries (through opinion campaigns, educational activities, prevention of illegality, crime suppression, etc.) (Fig. 2). Such initiatives can be geared toward stimulating security, pride, identity, and an "ethic of competitive trust" in a community — the social process by which it fortifies its capacity to successfully engage with the market.[6]

As can be seen, a very complex problem can be addressed from several complementary angles, brought together and set

---

[6] The responsible-direct relationship is valid in the case of provision of services rather than funding (because of the danger of "match-fixing" between administrative discretion and beneficiary initiative). In addition, it can stimulate citizen participation (thanks to the success of opinion campaigns, interactive education, combating *omertà*, etc.); but it does not include the process of involvement in box III, Fig. I (see below, points 12 and 13). Finally, it generally takes the form presented in box of Fig. 2 but is often aided by forms of responsible-indirect (or contextual) relationships. For example, good teaching requires the availability of a school, appropriate texts, etc. A particularly illuminating case in point is the contribution to crime reduction in New York City made by the fight against "disorder", which began with subway graffiti in the mid-1980s and then continued against non-ticket-paying, micro-crime etc. (Gladwell 1999, pp. 140-151).

in motion either simultaneously (in coordination) and/or successively, so as to suggest a favorable economic and social perspective.[7]

7. Finally, I hasten to add that the four cells (and their possible development) should not be used to cage the complexity of the real world. They are intended only as points of reference to reduce the level of illusion about human behavior often implied in various economic policy proposals. They should be consulted about what ought to be done and should stimulate our thinking accordingly.

In this way, on the basis of some simply outlined criteria, we can question *ab ovo* the more or less promising nature of a given policy intervention. This will be the case even if its order of magnitude turns out to be too feeble or too strong (to the point of becoming counterproductive); even if possible counter impulses — this is the case with linkages — may be generated by its implementation; and even if, in order to advance beyond this first step through educated guesswork, additional features of the concrete situation need to be considered.

Automatisms and "Distortions"
8. The six (dual) criteria in Fig. 1, chosen to organize intervention policies for the South, compose between them a complex of fifteen two-way relationships. We have chosen three of them, placed respectively in the cells on the left — automatic and indirect, responsible and with involvement, inducting for the public administration and for the beneficiaries — without, however, precluding access to others, because we believe that these are the most relevant. To clarify the point, we can briefly recall some of the reasoning that led us to identify them.

---

[7] This implies (among other things) the possibility of coordinating and using specific contributions from different actors sequentially and/or simultaneously. For example, the lesson on the economic effects of mafia organizations (Centorrino and Signorino, 1997) and the lesson on economic "fundamentals" (Aquino, 1996) should not be seen, in my opinion, as alternatives, but as complementary (cf. Part II of Meldolesi, 1992a).

In order to oppose the decline of Southernist policy, "Mezzogiorno, with Joy" called for a change in approach which, along with the restoration of the authority of the state and the proper functioning of public administrations, advocates the liberalization of markets, the gradual de-legalization of the special body of legislation for the Mezzogiorno, the de-nationalization of its economy, and the development of the Southern financial system — that is, the work of selecting and supporting private investment. The text also supports the need to reconvert a good part of the operation to automatic and indirect — "so as to produce a change in many ways analogous to what happens to the temptation to evade taxes when a self-emplyed worker becomes a wage earner with automatic withholding."[8]

To clarify, it might seem at first glance that there is no real difference in the ways a certain sum of money is spent — for example, issuing a check as opposed to reducing taxes and fees by the same amount for a beneficiary. Instead, the fact is that the indirect transfer is universalist (it reaches everyone who is in a certain condition), while the direct one can be "rationed" (usually due to scarcity of funds), in which case it prompts the individual — more or less consciously — to "go after" the financing. In other words, he or she may be "led into temptation" and use one of the thousands of traditional ways to curry favor with the powerful. It is a root of clientelism that can in fact be "dribbled" (to use a football metaphor), transforming its disbursement — from direct to indirect.

---

[8] See ch. 2 of this volume, p. 28. I do not, of course, refuse to discuss the question of "more or less government" specifically, when it comes to seeking the most satisfactory solution to a given problem. But as a general approach — as I explained in *Spender meglio* — I prefer to leave the determination of the level of public spending to Parliament and grapple with the related (or dual) task of its efficiency. My problem is to sort out the best state (and the best market), a public interest problem which, while based on my beliefs, transcends intransigence and can facilitate communication between traditionally opposing viewpoints.

The support measures that lend themselves to automatic and indirect use are actually numerous.[9] They include free services, tax relief for local authorities, reduction in the price of central public services (gas, electricity, railways), the reduction of the tax burden (direct and indirect), the taxation of social security charges, subsidized credit "across the board," etc. (Of course, not all should be placed on the same footing—for example, a tax exemption for reinvested profits certainly has a greater expansive effect than the taxation of social security contributions).

9. But we need to reflect for a moment on the behavioral consequences of such measures. It is not only a matter of freeing the beneficiary from the sort of clientelist subordination that creates a climate of dependence and waiting to be spoon-fed—with the resulting diversion and depression of productive energies. It is also about moving intelligently in the opposite direction through a psychological mechanism that by analogy with the "money illusion" of economic tradition I would like to christen the "indirect transfer illusion." Quite apart from clientelist channels that can be concealed (even at the psychological level), the recipient, while claiming (as commonly happens) that the funding is simply compensation for Southern handicaps—nevertheless cannot deny having received it. In contrast, those who get an indirect transfer of the same amount do not even notice it and can therefore *entirely* credit themselves for any economic success they may achieve, thus setting in motion (more easily) an important mechanism of psychological adaptation to the new condition. In fact, through dissonance (prompting the subjects to adapt when reality contradicts their thinking), meta-preferences and experience-based discernment, this allows for a gradual abandonment of the welfare

---

[9] The same can be said for automatic penalty measures that could be imposed for example on municipalities that do not properly collect social housing rents, garbage taxes, streetcar tickets, etc.

mentality and a hardening of the virtuous circle of work/increased productivity/income/ consumption, etc.[10]

More precisely, "Mezzogiorno, with Joy" — as mentioned — inserted the economic theory of the "optimal monetary area" of Scitovsky, Mundell and McKinnon into the social context of the South, concluding that the order of the three recommendations arising from that theory to enable the rebalancing of markets — wage differentiation, labor mobility and "automatisms" — must be reversed, because of the sociopolitical constraints affecting the former (and partly the latter) — constraints that, as subsequent history has since confirmed,[11] can be overcome only gradually. Moreover, within the automatic transfers proposed by that theory, "Mezzogiorno, with Joy" opted for indirect ones — as just mentioned. Finally, linking this result to that of *The Strategy*, it suggested automatic, indirect and behavior-inducing measures (as in boxes I and III of Fig. 1).

10. There is, however, a second constraint of a cultural and institutional nature. By definition, the measures recalled above would produce a "distortion" — economists would say — of resource allocation.[12] Hence the contrary opinion expressed by

---

10 Meldolesi 1992a, chs. 4 and 5; 1994b, pp. 104-111.

11 Cf., for example, the resistance that exists in the private sector to accepting contracts with wage differentials on a territorial basis. In the public sector only Antonio Aquino, to my knowledge, has so far advocated such a measure.

12 Reasoning from theory, the "distortionists" often argue that the only possible intervention in the South is in infrastructure because, referring to the environment within which productive activity takes place, this would not interfere with the allocation of resources. I confess that in terms of theory I am puzzled by this thesis at the level of general economic equilibrium because it amounts to treating infrastructure as public policy and not as fixed social capital (cf. Hulten 1994). But this is not my only misgiving. It also seems to me that this thesis is a shortcut to avoid the complex path (indicated later in the text) of estimating what these distortions would actually be and comparing them with the benefits of the action to be taken. Moreover, apart from the behavior problems that are actually very serious, it forgets that infrastructural works (and with them real services, professional courses, etc.) when they are a response to pressing needs and represent a gracious handout, have — if all goes well — a permissive function that is anything but an inducement to development.

the European Union and the current tendency to abandon this form of intervention.[13]

Personally, I am not convinced that this is reasonable. Firstly, the traditional inability of economics to understand the psychological-behavioral effects of policy intervention is reflected here in the failure to distinguish between forms of support related to the patronage system and forms that are exempt from it. In the second place, the general reorientation of the country has changed the atmosphere by allowing healthy Southern firms to take a step forward.[14] But a lack of support for them (automatic and indirect) could undermine their growth and proliferation.

And third, market distortions must be compared with the positive effects of the intervention. In this regard, it must be stressed that very little can be taken for granted and deduced *ex ante*. On one side of the scale one must place the shifts in the curves induced by the intervention together with the movements along these curves, which furthermore depend on their concretely detected elasticity. On the other side one has to consider the effect of the intervention, which has to be evaluated on a case-by-case basis. In many cases I consider it to be "backward sloping" in the sense that at too low a level it would barely be felt and at too high a level it would discourage efforts at improvement and end up being counterproductive. Between such extremes, the zone of "optimal imbalance" must be sought through a process of progressive approximation (trial and error).[15]

Let's take an example. If electricity were free of charge, there would surely be a very large shortfall for the treasury and

---

[13] In the past (Meldolesi 1993a) I have tried, without much success, to use European structural policies to reinvigorate the body and blood of the Sicilian regional administration. This does not mean, of course, that the measures that EU regional policy has financed so far in the Mezzogiorno are fully commendable (see, for example, Iannuzzo 1990 and Tagle 1992). It only means that, because of their characteristics (and importance), considerable progress is possible in this area.

[14] Cf., for example, Bàculo, ed.(1994), Bàculo (1997).

[15] Meldolesi (1994c).

a huge waste of energy, because the user would no longer have any interest in "flipping the light switch." Conversely, if the price of electricity were only marginally lower than the price due, the user would barely notice the benefit. In contrast, a substantial reduction in price, but not too much, would produce a corresponding transfer of income and encourage the initiation or bolstering of small, energy-consuming home manufacturing activities. Finally, the containment of total energy consumption could be pursued, for example, by linking the differential price of installed kilowatts to the free distribution of "environmentally friendly" light bulbs. In essence, those who want to pay very little should learn to use those bulbs if they want to run their washing machines.

11. On the other hand, policy interventions could also fall into the first cell at the top of Box III of Fig. 1, where the action of the public administration "induces" the beneficiary to act, while in turn the latter's initiative "induces" the action of others by way of linkage. In such a case, it would not only be true, as I have already mentioned,[16] that automatic support would represent a floor for economic actors to walk on ("without hindrance—that is, without having to engage in the exasperating search for a way in") and that such a floor would be as mobile as a conveyor belt. It would also be the case that the intervention, precisely because of its greater effectiveness/efficiency, would mutually affect the actors by making their emancipation process more expeditious.

The reasoning thus leads to a final point. It should never be forgotten that the practical economic policy we are trying to construct can be gradually "adjusted" through small variations, up or down, so as to identify the moving optimal range that is to be pursued, a step at a time. In this way, by means of incremental corrective processes, it is possible to make a judgment on each individual intervention by comparing the distorting aspects with those *factually verified* as propulsive and,

---

[16] And as I have written elsewhere: Meldolesi 1992a, p. 82; 1994a, p. 300.

in this way, choose the overall solution to be pursued. As in the case of the notion of optimal disequilibrium,[17] the distortion introduced by the intervention pushes the economy along a less efficient path. Successively, however, precisely because it calls up and enlists dormant capacities and resources for development, the impact of the measure produces a significant acceleration and thus enables significantly higher goals to be achieved — see Fig. 3.

FIGURE 3

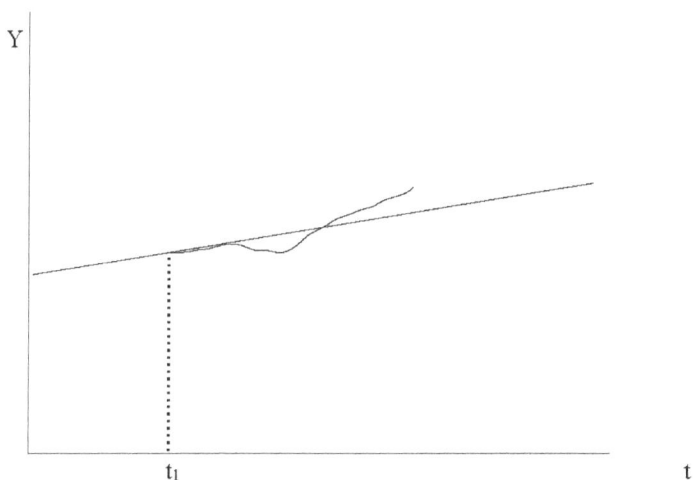

Key issues and clientelism
12. Having outlined (in part) the logic of labor, our focus returns to the automatic and indirect measures listed above. Connecting Boxes I and III of Fig. 1, we find that while some of these — such as free services, lower prices of public services, a lower indirect tax burden or an "across the board" reduction in the interest rate — belong in the first cell of Box I, they do not fit so much into the first cell of Box III as they do into the third — the one that pairs the inducing (in this case obligatory

[17] Hirschman and Lindblom 1962; Meldolesi 1994c

since it is automatic) of the administration with the permissive of the beneficiary. In fact, such measures enable higher incomes and lower production costs, respectively, for the households and operators who benefit from them. This happens *only* if these subjects desire it—there is no mechanism here that pushes them to act.

Other instruments, however, can be devised in such a way as to actually induce the beneficiaries to behave "virtuously": automatic and indirect relief to local authorities can be linked to objective indicators (services actually provided, budget balance, etc.), the partial detaxation of profits reinvested in the enterprise rewards and thus "induces" performance and investment, partial taxation of social security contribution "induces" employment growth—above-board employment, we should point out.

Furthermore, such behaviors may themselves be permissive (such as local authority services) or alternately permissive or inducing (in the other cases). Here one would need to go into specifics to study the groups of linkages (upstream, downstream, consumption, fiscal, cultural), their nature (permissive or inducing), their size and intensity, drawbacks, etc. This would be necessary for constructing a targeted action that in addition to belonging to the first cell in Box III, would also have the most positive effect on behavior and growth.

At the same time, the more we go into the details, the further away the reasoning moves from the simple and general logic of automatic and indirect support outlined above. This weighs against a "compression" of the framework for the sake of conciseness. The criteria of automatic-indirect and of inducing PA and inducing B, although connectable, need to remain distinct. The one will take the other into consideration for the purpose of discussing the fine-tuning of the intervention without abandoning its home soil.

Thus, if the prevailing concern is with behavior, the automatic-indirect criterion will also take inducing PA and inducing B into account. Conversely, if the reasoning emphasizes inducing mechanisms, it will also have to look into behavioral consequences since "the art of promoting development may therefore consist primarily in multiplying the opportunities to engage in these dissonance-arousing actions and in inducing an initial commitment to them"[18]

13. The question may be looked at from different points of view. To extricate oneself from the clientelist grip, it is possible to beat a path that lies in a sense at the opposite pole from the former — the criterion of responsible-with involvement.[19] Its initial formulation, in "Mezzogiorno, with Joy," was in the context of carefully evaluated development projects set up by people held responsible for the results — from design to proper management of the facility.

Cases like this are unfortunately rare in the Mezzogiorno. There is however the experience of youth entrepreneurship (law 44/1986). The only surviving part of the Intervento Straordinario, it created hundreds of businesses led by young entrepreneurs thanks to a high level of state participation in start-up investments. This was combined with an ingenious procedure which, starting with the evaluation of the project, propelled the would-be entrepreneur into a close relationship with the management entity. Through successive funding deadlines and their

---

[18] Hirschman (1971) p. 325.

[19] The criteria of automatic-indirect and responsible-with involvement define two solid extremes of a spectrum that is otherwise brittle (cf. Meldolesi 1992a, pp. 71, 87-88 and 91-92). They are linked by an inversion relation in the sense (often found in interactive thinking) that one is related to the other as its opposite. (Automatic is obligatory for the administration and thus is the opposite of discretionary, which is itself necessary if the employee is to be held responsible for the results; indirect is the opposite of direct — which is indispensable for the involvement of the recipient. Vice versa, involvement is the opposite of the non-involvement typical of indirect measures, while someone responsible for the consequences of their own actions is the opposite of the non-responsible person who simply performs a required act). This is a retrospective observation, however, because the two pairings examined here arose from observation of reality and reflection on experience. Automatic-indirect as an adjunct and counterweight to the push for liberalization was from the outset an inspiring aspect of "Mezzogiorno, with Joy." Responsible-with involvement instead grew in stages as a result of integrating into the initial text the results achieved in the writings that would eventually make up chapters 3, 4, 1, and 6 of *Spender meglio è possibile* (and then Meldolesi 1993, 1994d, and Meldolesi and Stame 1995).

monitoring, beneficiary participation in the funding (smaller but substantial), training courses, assignment of a mentor, etc., the beneficiary was (increasingly) involved, pushed to face obstacles that *ex ante* were unknown or underestimated, persuaded to adapt his or her thinking to the new conditions and thus to actually act as an entrepreneur—until, having survived the "incubation" period, he or she was in a position to take wing.

This process of involvement and transformation brought with it the assumption of a high level of accountability on the part of the Committee (later transformed into a youth entrepreneurship company and finally incorporated into Sviluppo Italia). The committee-company examined 4,000 projects through iterative processes that led to 13,000 evaluations. It also devised a reasonable selection process for young people's business ideas so as to follow the protocol for the number of applications without experiencing substantial delays. This made it possible to avoid the danger of finance rationing, which would have made the many individual referrals more effective.[20]

14. The civil servant's responsibility cannot be to ensure that assisted enterprises run smoothly—the job is to assist the young entrepreneurs in managing their businesses, not replace them. Nevertheless, as is generally the case for employees in countries that have reformed their administrations, the responsibility of these officials must be accountability for their own actions in the sense of an orientation toward results, rather

---

[20] Clearly this observation captures only one aspect of an experience (inevitably) affected by the era in which it was envisioned. Unfortunately, the prevailing business culture within the committee-company for young entrepreneurship, and even more so in the other companies that made up Sviluppo Italia did not include actual knowledge of the area (Southern light industrialization, local development, the underground economy, etc.). On the contrary, it seems to presuppose a lack of initiative in the South that, fortunately, is not at all widespread. In addition, the measures referred to in the text have failed to fully take hold. Self-referential and parasitic practices have unfortunately also spread into Sviluppo Italia, so that after a period of anxious anticipation, a certain disappointment with the institution's behavior has prevailed in public opinion.

than the notion (widely prevalent in our country) of mere formal respect for procedures. For example, the official must actively collaborate with the management of the assigned company, doing what is possible (rather than the minimum required) in the company's interests, promptly reporting any problems and dysfunctions and working intelligently to correct them, and so on. In short, they should not just care, they should actively work toward reaching the best possible outcome (in their own work, and as an indirect consequence also for their assigned company).

The general sense of the example is clear. In fact one need only look at some of the titles in a key text from the movement for state reform—Osborne and Gaebler's *Reinventing Government*, the basis of Gore's report of the same name[21] —to grasp in an instant the general frame in which such an approach might take off: steering rather than rowing, empowering rather than serving, handing out assignments rather than rules, funding outcomes rather than inputs, meeting the client's needs ... and so on.

Outline and outlook
15. If at this point, in order to explore our framework further, we were to link the logic of Box II with that of Box III in Fig. 1, we would find ourselves reasoning along lines similar to those explored above.

The companies under law 44/1986 were "induced" by the provision of funding, while they in their turn had differing effects—inducing and/or permissive—on the economy. It cannot be ruled out that in the concrete operation of the committee-company for youth entrepreneurship this question actually came up occasionally, nor can it be ruled out that it could play a greater role in a clearer and more comprehensive economic policy framework. Still, if the issue were to gain preeminence it would end up altering the spirit of the initiative, which is

---

[21] Osborne and Gaebler 1992; Gore 1993.

precisely to support viable projects that can break through the subordinate economic equilibrium of this less developed area.

So, we arrive at the conclusion that the two types of measures resistant to "welfarism" — the automatic and indirect type and the responsible and with involvement type — much as they can be linked to Box III in Fig. 1, cannot and should not be transposed in terms of inducing PA and inducing B analysis. On the contrary, albeit asymmetrically (since the automatic-indirect rationale is general in nature, while the responsible-with involvement rationale is *ad personam*), the fact is that the "anticlientelist level" of reasoning indirectly delimits an entire field of pathological risk into which different forms of intervention often fall [...].

16. It is thus worthwhile to move in the opposite direction and examine these forms in relation to what is suggested in Boxes I and II of our outlines. This makes it clear that the part of the special intervention which in the 1960s and 1970s undertook to analyze connections and degrees of freedom for poor performance (which can be considered the *cardum* and *decumanum* of Albert Hirschman's entire construction [Meldolesi 1995, p. 161.]) not only did so in a narrow and partial way, it did not even dream — this is the truth — of raising the underlying motivational and behavioral issues.[22]

So that when I began my search for a new economic policy for the Mezzogiorno, in a generally oppressive climate that presaged the great collapse of the Intervento Straordinario, I couldn't help but adopt a viewpoint alternative to the current way of thinking. The intention of "Mezzogiorno, with Joy" was

---

[22] Unfortunately, acknowledgment of this aspect of the completed intervention has not been forthcoming. There is the beginning of a discussion concerning linkages — on the scarcity of upstream links in particular, and on the need to look also at non-productive connections (consumer, fiscal, cultural). But as far as I know, the first attempt to trace any such effects in the field is the one started by Rosanna Bussoletti in her thesis on 3M in Caserta (1996). As for the question of the wide or narrow degree of freedom for poor performance it is largely outside the cultural scope of Southern economists.

in fact to promote the creative revival of the theme of *The Strategy of Economic Development* in light of detailed field studies.

17. I believe therefore that the practical research of the working group at the University of Naples that I coordinated together with Liliana Bàculo—for example, on the "uncertainties" of the small entrepreneur, on the constellation of events favorable to the birth of enterprises, on the *humus* that sustains certain local systems, on successful companies, on the territorial structure of the Southern economy, on large companies in the South— can (and should) be aimed at identifying targeted measures, defined in their various aspects and thus behaviorally verified both from the automatic-indirect side and from the responsible-with involvement side.

This will require questioning the reasons both for the significant steps forward that we witnessed and for their limitations—examining where the positive and negative dimensions are closely linked and can be analyzed in alteration, taking opposite positions. Thus, the danger of "getting stuck," which rounds out the best-known sequential analysis of linkages,[23] suggests we construct suture points between different sequential processes. Similarly, research on degrees of freedom—- both inside projects and companies, ranging between narrow and broad, and external, between voice and exit[24]—may be carried out starting from the positive side[25] or from the negative side—that is, studying how an internal and/or external targeted intervention could lead to efficiency recovery in a given production environment.

Finally, a historical study of the Intervento Straordinario[26] can set up a useful background for the new frontiers of our research and help us come to grips with the regional policy of the European Union.

---

[23] Hirschman 1995, chs. 2, 3 and 5.
[24] I am referring here to the line of thinking starting in chapter 8 of *The Strategy* (cf. Meldolesi 1995, pp. 154-157).
[25] As in Tagle 1994.
[26] As in Bianchi 1999.

Tools

18. One additional word. I would like to reverse the direction of the reasoning and focus on administration, referring at the same time to some remedies that have been suggested.[27] To this end, I would like to turn to that part of S. Lester Salamon's work[28] that emphasizes the tools of government action.[29]

Can the view presented here perhaps be said to imply the acceptance of such an instrumental approach, rather than the better-known approaches that focus on government agencies, or public policies or their enactment (so-called implementation)? In part, yes, but in part this is not the case.

On one side of the scale, I would put my own interest in such tools.[30] In "automatic and indirect" cases, it is a matter of finding ways of achieving the desired results that are quick and easy as well as effective and efficient in the forms most suitable for the user and with the lowest administrative costs. In the "responsible and with involvement" cases, besides the features indicated above, the different experiences would need to be explored comparatively to bring out their advantages and limitations, identify possible variants, etc.

In both, even while aiming to stabilize the general plan of the policy pursued, minute revisions will have to be made at regular intervals so as to constantly adjust actual practice to the desired ends. Moreover, above this "material base," a targeted intervention of a new kind will have to be developed — one that is "light" (in cost and apparatus), mobile, capable of timely results, and able to operate in this or that sector of the chessboard; an intervention that is continually evaluated and

---

[27] This allows us also to mention the decision-making process that takes place upstream from the administration — and thus to open (perhaps in a second moment) a path similar to the one that leads from *The Strategy* to *Journeys* (Meldolesi 1995, ch. 2-4).

[28] Salamon, ed., 1989.

[29] This text was pointed out to me by Laura Tagle.

[30] To continue with the analogy indicated in note 12, it is noteworthy that Albert Hirschman's "microtechnological" approach, referred to in this paper, is particular both to the line of thinking from *The Strategy* and the line concerning the "style" of policy-making that comes from *Journeys* (Meldolesi 1995, pp. 83-85, 91-93).

refined, and managed by capable people who are responsible for the results obtained. For all these reasons tool interests me, and therefore its dimensions — such as those that concern the nature of the measures to be taken, the structure of the actions they require, the degree of centralization, the consequences, how automatic they are, etc. Indeed, I think some deeper reflection on the issues examined by Salamon[31] would allow us to begin to turn the suggestions outlined here into comprehensive proposals.

19. On the other side of the scale I have to put our differences. In the first place, my point of view is more general because it includes the reaction of the beneficiaries—this is a downstream extension that (as I mentioned in note 26) can extend upstream as well. In addition, my approach is more specific because it is constructed to begin with the problems rather than the tools.

I do not question the advantages and disadvantages of a certain tool in general, because I am simply looking for the tool that best corresponds to a particular goal. And in the same way that I think that there is no single road to achieving a given result—indeed the diagram suggests combining several sets of different roads—I also think that there is no best tool. There is a multiplicity of tools with advantages and disadvantages that must be weighed, tried and tried again—not least in combination with each other—to gradually achieve better results.

Finally, my interest in the tool is not exclusionary. In the ongoing search for the "best," the reasoning also spontaneously brings in different aspects of government agencies as well as the policies pursued and their enactment, precisely those aspects that Salamon would instead like to keep separate...

---

[31] Salamon, ed., 1989, pp. 34-42, 46.

8. Basic Outline for an Emergence Project*

For a long time, undeclared and semi-submerged workers and economic activity of the South have been kept at the margins of Italian life. Only in recent years have they attracted the interest of public opinion, sparking a debate that has resulted (among other things) in a vote favoring regularization in the Senate of the Republic. To briefly survey the gulf that stretches between such deliberations and the factual reality of things, the following pages will explore the logical underpinnings and main provisions of a possible emergence project agreed upon with the European Union.

Foreword
Southern submerged economic activity has greater solidity in the plains (the flesh) than in the hills (the bone). This has to do with the different aspects of producing goods and services: local units, labor, production, export, wages, profits, etc. Such activity is generally exercised by small, family-run enterprises. The form it takes is more of semi-submersion (and double accounting) than of submersion *tout court*. It is present in different gradations in much of the private sector, hinging on the mobility, flexibility, cooperation, and intensity of informal labor. The salaries it pays vary greatly, from 300-400 thousand lire a month up to a million and more. Sometimes it is time-based and sometimes piecework (with higher wages). In some regions it constitutes the prevailing condition. In the South it (probably) accounts for

* From Meldolesi, L. (2022), *Protagonismi mediterranei*, pp. 47-64. Originally published in Del Prete, E., Mariti, P. and Vellere, M.A. (eds.) (1998), "L'economia italiana tra centralità europea e marginalità mediterranea" [The Italian economy between European centrality and Mediterranean marginality]. This memoir, presented at the National Conference on Emplyment (Bari, 1996) emerged from a discussion which involved the participation at various times of Valeria Aniello, Nicola Campoli, Alberto Carzaniga, Alberto De Crais, Giuliano Sciarri and Nicoletta Stame.

the majority of the work actually performed, while in the country as a whole it is estimated as a quarter, a third or more. Along with struggling businesses, it is characterized by productive activities that enjoy good health that are often part of district-oriented concentrations of incipient light industrialization in the South. (Goods for the home or the person in small batches, produced for third parties or in-house, through flexible specialization—or versatile integration—for domestic and international markets, part of the well-known Made in Italy system).

2. At the same time that this situation was coming to light, the idea was put forward that the primary way to increase the frequency of regular work was above all the full emergence of the economy of the Mezzogiorno. This appears consistent, moreover, with other important goals: the affirmation of legality, the economic consolidation and social rehabilitation of the South, the legitimization of republican institutions, the fight against petty and organized crime, etc.

Furthermore, the European Union's official view, which draws on current regional policy, would suggest increasing labor mobility and wage flexibility. However, the latter would have to be truly dramatic in the South to push the entire sector toward emergence. Namely, given current norms, it would have to allow for wages far lower than the lowest undeclared wages at present.[1]

Thus, there is a danger that despite the consensus achieved

---

[1] This is not to question the need to deviate *pro tempore* from the working conditions prevailing in the rest of the country, but only to point out that beyond a certain threshold, under normal democratic conditions, such deviation will meet increasing obstacles. It does not seem entirely reasonable to entrust the comparative recovery of the Mezzogiorno solely to the instrument of wage flexibility. (In addition, a similar conclusion also seems justified from another point of view. In the literature, the level of submersion is often correlated directly with the tax and contribution "wedge" and indirectly to the degree of repression. In both respects, the road today appears to be uphill. Regarding the "wedge," the reduction of pressure in the short term appears daunting for sure, and regarding repression, after a few clumsy attempts, the attitude that seems prevalent today—for how long is uncertain—is one of wait and see).

and a number of favorable elements (such as the opening of the new political phase enabled by the end of the Cold War and developments in the European integration process), emergence will fail to take hold—with very negative consequences for the effective functioning of the country. Suffice it to recall that Italian budget revenues are inequitably distributed among taxpayers, or that in spite of our political and trade union traditions, the undocumented Southern worker is treated worse than the most mistreated worker in America or Japan.[2]

3. The implementation of an emergence project agreed upon with European authorities thus appears to be the most reasonable option from several points of view.

Nevertheless (and first and foremost), it has to answer a current objection. If taxation of social security contributions —some observers reason—were distorting competition, why should the same criticism not be directed at a project of emergence?

Fortunately, the problem is badly framed.[3] Fortunately, the liberation of productive forces promised by European integration cannot be turned on its head as a final condemnation of the South to live in a state of apnea. The truth, instead, is that such fears reveal a lack of familiarity with the workings of Europe, a doubt about our future direction that we must quickly overcome.

---

[2] The productive activity of small businesses in Japan benefits from a general exception in labor law. In the United States there is nothing more than a relatively contained minimum wage. But in both these countries, in contrast with Italy, such activity is legal. Small businesses and their workers have nothing to be afraid of — they are not forced to hide their work situation. The bottom line is that while we need to recognize our own "indecency," we also should cherish the legitimate ambition to create a better world of work for everyone than the one Japanese and American workers currently enjoy.

[3] In retrospect, it must be acknowledged that Italy's entire social-political culture has been subjected to the European viewpoint on the taxation of social security contributions without really understanding it. Instead of looking to uncover the vast Southern submerged economy, the preference has often been to question the economic theory at the foundation of the argument, maintaining instead that as a consequence the abolition of the taxation would favor further submersion.

Indeed, the concern raised above, that those regional policies, labor mobility, and wage flexibility will fail to propel the Mezzogiorno toward a re-balancing within a reasonable time horizon poses a serious problem for both us and Europe. This in a twofold sense—because the failure of the recovery mechanism in the South weakens the foundations of the whole European construction, and because, as we hear every day, businesses are using the underground economy as a competitive weapon. If anything, it is this that *distorts* competition, certainly not the project constructed to overcome it.

It is thus clear that the long concealment of the reality of the Southern shadow economy out of misguided pride or guile has seriously damaged the interests of the South, the country and the European construction itself.[4] It is time to turn the page. What is needed is a project of emergence that sets out to lead the Mezzogiorno as quickly as possible to the regularization, legalization and thus Europeanization of its economy—a plan that will expire with the convalescence of the subject and will suggest similar paths to other somewhat distracted owners of the European household.

The Rationale of the Outline: Local Action
4. All this surely clarifies the *philosophy* of the present proposal, whose aim is a new drive for the integration of the Mezzogiorno. Like the continent's move toward monetary union, it could set in motion an effective mechanism for the rapid liberation of the South. Such a mechanism would finally create the conditions that would attract external capital to the Mezzogiorno, starting a process of full development.

---

[4] Transferred to the problem of the submerged economy, the reader will recognize here the point of view developed by Giovanni Falcone and Paolo Borsellino in their fight against organized crime. The disgrace, they explained, lies not in recognizing the existence of these serious social phenomena, but in tolerating them and thus accepting them as enduring and inevitable.

The project for emergence discussed below thus takes on a broader significance than the small scale of Southern businesses would suggest. It recognizes that there is an opportunity in the intense and proactive work going on in them that is different from the so-called welfarism that has prevailed in the recent past. Their direct and indirect strengthening can have positive consequences for the overall development of Southern society, because it rewards work, diligence, merit, and saving.[5]

The emergence project brings together many economic policy ideas that taken singly cannot produce the desired result, but when used in succession or jointly can have significantly greater impact. In other words, the present proposal does not aim for a legislative quick fix that gives the illusion of having plugged the leaks. It instead rests on the idea that emergence can result from the interplay of a complex of operations covering a wide arc of problems. To this end, its line of reasoning is organized into two chapters that we can call local direct action and centralized action, which is primarily indirect.

5. Traditionally, direct intervention is the main instrument of development policy. In the Mezzogiorno, after the cancellation of the Intervento Straordinario, development proceeded in the usual ways. In addition, at the urging of the European Community, a series of policies were devised at the local level — structural funds, territorial agreements, area, program, and training contracts, etc. The difficulties faced by this sector represent the tip of the iceberg of a more general administrative

---

[5] One of the great difficulties for social change and industrialization in the Mezzogiorno is likely in the fact that the part of the economy that has emerged and is benefiting from public funding often has welfarist tendencies of "aristocratic" origin, while the semi-submerged part, heir of craft and peasant traditions, unfortunately has one foot in illegality. The emergence project, by modifying the balance between the two sectors, could set in motion an important social as well as economic evolution, strengthening positive currents that are already present today.

inadequacy that urgently needs to be remedied.

The emergence project therefore starts here—from the need to bring about an administrative leap forward. While large-scale corruption has probably faded in recent years, the same cannot be said for *ordinary* corruption. Moreover, clientelism continues to play a significant role, while free-riding, wastefulness and neglect still thrive in the Southern climate of public inefficiency. Finally, due to submission to regulations, administration has essentially ground to a halt.

We must find the strength to get out of this situation, starting with "unblocking," which means first and foremost transitioning from today's system of final accounting to the industrial-style operational accounting now predominantly used in the contemporary world. This allows (among other things) identification of the areas of greatest inefficiency in the administrations and the launch of a reorganization aimed at increasing service, reducing personnel, or both. Moreover, such downsizing from the culture of regulation[6] in favor of a culture of figures, results and transparency may be a prelude to exploiting the leap in technology. By transforming the current use of information technology, a kind of mechanization of what already exists, into a true web-based system that concentrates all information in a single database and allows it to be cross-correlated, it is possible to radically change the way service is produced and enormously increase the productivity of work.

Italian public administration is accustomed to constant or even waning productivity. But we are entering an era of sustained and continuous productivity growth in the sector. In

---

[6] More precisely, in tune with the reorganization of the 160,000 regulations into single texts envisaged by the Bassanini reform (the European average is 6,000 regulations), what we propose here is to concentrate in a single legal department all the regulatory compliance activity that today predominates in all administrative units and actually impedes their economic functioning.

this process the problem that arises everywhere is how to overcome administrative Fordism and change the DNA—as Al Gore's advisor David Osborne (1992) argues—"banishing" the bureaucratic in favor of the five levers of *Reinventing Government*—purpose, incentives, accountability, empowerment and culture.

6. Southern administrations also have to fit into the mainstream of the contemporary world; the emergence project we are trying to outline must include a sustained and continuous increase in the productivity of administrative work as measured by operational accounting. It is an operational change that can revitalize local government and bring order to the many projects it is involved in. In particular, regions, provinces and municipalities have a very poor mastery of the measures that are undertaken and the overall framework they help to create. Normally, at the urging of one sort of pressure or another, a series of decisions is made, the consequences of which then unfold "out of sight." This is a phenomenon that is all the more pronounced the larger the human and territorial universe involved and the smaller the public interest in it.

It is again a matter of reversing the trend—of seeking coordination and synergy among operations by activating practical planning efforts based on actual knowledge of the situation. Simple implementation procedures need to be put in place that establish priorities and alternative advantages (trade-offs), and that exploit first and foremost the projects with the greatest revenue growth, perhaps involving other actors, the financial system, etc. Finally, it is essential to put in place both a monitoring mechanism linked to operational accounting and a follow-up of *ex post* evaluation as a basis for the recurrent reorganization of the different policy interventions.

7. The overall goal of these activities—this is our claim—must be emergence. This means first and foremost taking an active interest in factual reality, instead of the self-blindfolding that has been going on up to now.[7]

Moreover, such knowledge must underpin conscious policy interventions. Consider, first of all, the creation of Area Service Centers which, in collaboration with craft and business associations and starting from the simplest aspects (tax and technical advice, information on financing opportunities, etc.) aim at an effective upgrading of existing entrepreneurship.[8]

These include the simplification and fairness of administrative procedures, the system of incentives whose use should be carefully evaluated, the creation of businesses with public money, which awaits timelier sectoral and territorial applications,[9] the complex issue of unfinished or poorly managed public works, the question of new projects, etc.

8. Experience shows that direct intervention suffers from the pressing danger of diversion of public money to other purposes.[10] To be properly managed it requires a high degree of

---

[7] Alluding to the current practice of various public measures that are calibrated as if the informal economy did not exist, it so happens that the job of business start-ups not only follows existing legislation as a matter of course but assumes that the businesses created will behave properly in the future. Instead, it turns out from field investigations that the permitted investments, the expected level of employment, etc. are subsequently adapted to the conditions of the dual market—the regular and the irregular. Are these enterprises not taught to seek corporate profit?

[8] In fact, the spontaneous incentive to emerge exists not only in the labor force. As the history of light industrialization in the North-Center shows, the very momentum of development and the strengthening of small businesses places on them a need for progressive regularization (in order to access financing, to con-solidate business relations, to be able to export, to get administrative licenses, etc.).

[9] Triggered by the assumption of a shortage of entrepreneurship, this type of intervention (for reasons mentioned in n. 7) should be redirected toward a consolidation and development of existing semi-submerged entrepreneurship, limiting *ex novo* creation to areas that actually lack it and to those areas where inroads are necessary.

[10] Due to intellectual limitations that do not allow them to study the effects of different interventions on human behavior, economists have often underestimated

accountability on the part of the officials, who must be organized along task force lines. And it also requires a high and progressive involvement on the part of the beneficiaries who, attracted by the available funds, must be encouraged through a wide variety of expedients to actually play the required entrepreneurial role. When this twofold condition is relaxed or fails, the danger of misuse of funding grows accordingly. It is therefore essential to reverse the burden of proof and require that the relevant organizing laws contain convincing prevention and disqualification mechanisms in this regard.

Connecting this point with that of reforming the public administration reveals the inspiration for our proposal—a state friendly to the emergence and development of the South must not get played. Only in this way can it hope to trigger a positive spiral of growth of labor productivity in the public administration and the Southern economy and gradually, through intensive and extensive accumulative processes, mobilize the latent energies of the Mezzogiorno.

The Government Action
9. What should be done at the Center to support and promote the process of emergence? Several things are indispensable. First, the administrative change in the periphery is obviously facilitated by a similar process at headquarters. If nothing else, the peripheral organs of the state have an important role to play (fiscal, social security, law and order). The process of emergence is

---

this problem. Nevertheless, as the experience of the Mezzogiorno shows, an administrative system that is unable to keep track of the consequences of its decisions is likely to achieve results that differ greatly from those budgeted for, even when the funding actually reaches the intended recipient. In fact, it is likely that through a kind of psychological displacement, the repetition of such measures prompts the entrepreneur to divert energies from the private pursuit of profit in order to specialize in capturing public funding—to the point of becoming a semi-assisted figure. This is why successful entrepreneurs from the South often remark that they did not take that route—i.e., they did not receive (direct) public funding.

also a process of legitimizing institutions and thus building a new relationship of trust between administration and citizens that requires the active participation of the center. Take public order as an example. The priority of the fight against organized crime in past years has had the unfortunate side effect of a persistently high level of common and petty crime. This is a serious handicap for productive activity in the Mezzogiorno and it is essential to tackle it—submersion is claimed as a defense against crime.

The South needs a very careful and determined law and order policy that assumes the perspective of small-scale production and the citizen. This means (among other things) protecting industrial zones, increasing external services outside relative to those inside offices, prosecuting crimes without exposing the victims to retaliation and revenge, creating public-private coordination structures with the participation of different forms of associated life (political, religious, youth) to combat drugs, petty crime, etc.

Such an initiative could keep a daily check on the situation in a particular area and would be supported by a small amount of funding linked to the emergence project. It could also be based on an iterative and incremental procedure—that is, on the evaluation of results and predetermined deadlines and the redirection and intensification of a project "calibrated" to the overall goal of legalization and social rehabilitation.

10. This brings us to the heart of the issue.[11] The center undoubtedly plays a very important role in stimulating and guiding the

---

[11] It should be noted in this regard that the following pages cannot be taken out of the context in which they are embedded. In other words—as we cautioned in sec. 4—the problem cannot be solved by a stand-alone technical maneuver. The latter, in our opinion, can be successful only within a large collective effort—i.e., a very large project clearly designed and carefully documented as it unfolds.

process of southern development as the focal point of this process. It must operate an indirect (and automatic) socioeconomic mechanism which, interacting with the direct (and discretionary) machinery discussed up to now, powerfully promotes the emergence of productive ventures. By lifting the myriad Southern businesses as if with a great collective hand, the center can propel them into confrontation with the regular market. This triggers a virtuous economic, social and even psychological action-reaction mechanism that is indispensable for getting the Mezzogiorno to stand on its own feet.[12]

Not all existing businesses will be able to cope successfully with such a transitional phase. It is in the logic of things for emerging light industrialization to go through processes of restructuring, merging, thinning, etc. But it is not just that. Along with the submerged Made in Italy — based, to be clear, on obvious craft skills — there is also in the South a poor underground economy that produces standardized goods in competition with Third World countries and pays starvation wages. In our view, while the former should be encouraged and consolidated through emergence, the latter should be extinguished through appropriate policies in the combined interests of the South and competing countries.[13]

---

[12] Unlike what was alluded to in n. 10, indirect and automatic intervention takes place "behind the back" of the entrepreneurs, who will have no need of any political *entrée*. Not only that: they will perceive the support as earned and will be able to take credit for the results achieved, setting in motion a mechanism of self-esteem that is very useful for overcoming the sense of inadequacy to the task that is so typical of the Southern condition.

[13] This is a decisive part of anti-poverty policy. To understand how little our country has done so far in this regard, it is enough to recall that the Ad Hoc Commission of the Prime Minister Office has simply reworked the available Istat data over the years. No door-to-door research on households has been done--a complete absurdity, as one senior IMF official commented privately.

11. The great process of change advocated here undoubtedly calls for a central orchestra conductor reporting directly to the Council Presidency. The idea is to have a very authoritative working group of technicians on short-term renewable contracts (so that they are kept on only if their work is actually indispensable), dedicated to the implementation, monitoring, evaluation, and planned redirection of the emergence policy.

The relationship between submersion and emergence is by its very nature unstable—it depends on the policies pursued, market trends and relative affordability as ascertained by a very large number of entrepreneurs. For example, last October's (1997) confirmation of the abolition of the taxation of social security contributions negatively affected the expectations of entrepreneurs, producing a strong impulse toward submersion that brought very serious unforeseen consequences. These ranged from the undermining of much of the progress that had been achieved in past years either spontaneously or through "gradual contracts" (an important page of contemporary union history affecting more than 30,000 workers), to the erosion of the Social Security base, to problems with the public budget. Moreover, as the months went by, the phenomenon of submersion began to expand even in the Center and North of the country, almost as if bad money were driving out good.

It is therefore essential to reverse the trend. Thoughts run to social security and tax relief of every type and degree, labor legislation, differential pricing of public services, etc.

In this regard, it is possible to construct a dual mechanism. On the one hand, of concessions that meet the needs of small producers, and on the other, for improvements in the public machinery of control that elevate the risk of being "caught."[14]

---

[14] To this end, it is essential to bring the various public administration databases on online so as to have a comprehensive view of citizens' activities (residences, cars, pensions, etc.). In particular, three tools should be built immediately: a telematic land

It is sufficient to state here the basic principles of this part of the emergence project.

a)   The impact especially at the beginning must be high, otherwise it would be impossible to reverse the current negative trend. While we have talked so far about better utilization of existing resources, it now becomes necessary to find additional resources. It would make sense if without detracting from the prerogatives of each region a portion of European structural funds were channeled in this direction along with other residuals that need to be carefully surveyed and deployed.

b)   Such a policy change must be part of a credible and formal country commitment agreed upon with EU authorities, such that it changes the expectations of both the operators and our partners. To this end, the proposed technical mechanism must be designed to provide for an action-reaction relationship that ensures absolute transparency and leads to successive decisions of redirection towards the goal to be achieved.

c)   Not least in order to distance themselves from the past, the measures in question should not be homogeneous for the entire Mezzogiorno. They may be differentiated by territorial, sectoral and labor conditions — for example, with respect to provincial unemployment rates, the types of production to be protected or promoted, specific labor figures, etc. The fine-tuning and ongoing verification of such a mechanism requires careful research work in the

---

registry in collaboration with the municipalities, a central telematic registry of the databases of the Social Security and Labor Offices, the DMV, Police, Public Health, building and business licenses, telephones, energy, etc. This would give a complete overview of the relationship between the state and the citizen, a reorganization of the tax registry which, in connection with previous projects, would allow the construction of an up-to-date and automatic socio-economic picture of each taxpayer.

field (to reflect concrete conditions as closely as possible) and close consultation with Brussels (to liaise with EU legislation). But, within reasonable limits, they involve simple procedures that can be centrally operated.

d)   The proposed measures must have agreed upon deadlines. Year by year verification of the emergence achieved may lead to a suspension of the operation (because it is ineffective), its intensification, or its tapering off until it is completely exhausted. This can also take place through a broadening of part of the measures to the entire country.

e)   The emergence project must enter into a synergistic relationship with policies promoting market flexibility and reduction of the tax burden. On the one hand, based on what was mentioned above, it is clear that the project will benefit from increasing flexibility and will come to an end when it is fully established.[15] On the other hand, the project aspires to trigger a virtuous circle that eventually enables the reduction of tax rates and in doing so also strengthens the push for emergence. To this end, it is possible to gradually reduce the Southern welfare apparatus (subsidies, old-age pensions, mobile workers, socially useful workers, etc.) — which functions as a "cornerstone" for the undeclared.[16] More precisely, launching the process of emergence makes it possible to channel labor into regular

_____

[15] In this respect, a mechanism could be considered for combining the advantages of stability and those of change. Each company could have a small percentage of a totally flexible workforce, a much higher percentage of a stable workforce and a third percentage in an intermediate condition. The unemployed could be automatically enrolled in a telematic marketplace but would lose unemployment benefits if they refused a job on offer.

[16] It is well known that a great many undeclared workers receive a government subsidy as an integral part of their income. While a drastic reduction in this subsidy appears socially difficult today, the triggering of a mechanism of emergence that favors a consolidation of businesses through increased investment, labor productivity and wages could make it feasible gradually to reduce the existing provision. See following n.

employment, so that the influence of these social shock absorbers is automatically diminished. Moreover, the regularization of working conditions would allow the gradual liquidation of the mechanism itself.[17]

12. The emergence project requires a conscious and intense effort. Its success depends crucially on the ability to mobilize local energies, using a credible and effective central point of reference. To carry out such a task (and support the federalist drive) the state must therefore be equipped.[18]

The state can actively facilitate the functioning of markets — labor, subcontracting, goods and services purchased by the public administration, etc. — through the establishment of telematic networks, perhaps supported by that of the Chambers of Commerce. In addition, it can initiate the decriminalization of many offenses committed in the course of normal

---

[17] The CIG (unemployment insurance) and all other forms of income support for the unemployed could be replaced with a decreasing, limited-time monthly allowance. A rent supplement tied to certain indicators monitored annually could be introduced. The pooling of pensions could be prevented and retirees encouraged to work. An effective direct assistance project could be launched (like food stamps) for all the poor and dispossessed, etc. In other words, a systematic policy of liberalization (and essential protection for those who really need it) could be pursued that makes sense in a context of the broader liberalization of numerous protected categories. Why do Italian pharmacies, for example, as Richard Freeman asked, resemble boutiques?

[18] For example, with the development of industrial-type accounting; with the launching of an integrated telematics system that would effectively allow the tax and fiscal behavior of its citizens to be monitored (see, n. 14 above); with a VAT reform that favors emergence, etc. (As things stand, VAT reform through the introduction of contrast of interests can only have an experimental and reiterative value. It should provide for a deduction from Irpef [income tax] only for certain categories of taxpayers and expenditures and should be fine-tuned at regular intervals based on the results achieved. For example, full deduction with a 10% premium for a maximum annual amount, for invoices entered in advance at the beneficiary's expense in the database of the tax registry through authorized terminals, credit institutions, financial operators and insurance companies, administrative offices, etc.).

economic activity and replace them with arbitration commissions which, in a climate of common sense and gradualness, could resolve the sort of disputes between businesses and the administration that stifle economic activity and are at the root of countless cases of corruption.

As for emergence in the true sense, the state can establish a specific procedure which, in exchange for the above-mentioned concessions, also institutes telematic audits and the registration of clients, suppliers and employees—a procedure accompanied, however, by complete impunity with respect to the past. Finally, it is necessary to implement in stages, starting with the most relevant issues, environmental, workplace safety, and labor rights legislation. Regarding the first two of these, it is well known that the transposition of EU directives has imposed administrative and financial burdens on craft enterprises that have reinforced the tendency to submerge. Regarding the third, there are survey data that show how in the South the regularization of employment relationships is prevented by the use that employees often make of newly acquired rights. Getting jobs into compliance should become synonymous with business consolidation and productive momentum—it should not be the antechamber of bankruptcy.

13. We have sought in this chapter to call together and briefly present the terms of the problem. Additional aspects may be added later. But already the picture thus drawn represents a formidable challenge for the near future of our country, one that will engender mixed feelings. On the one hand, it is an opportunity to see a process of emancipation finally deployed, a process capable of mobilizing positive energies, especially among young people. On the other, there is the danger that the explication of the economic, political and social conditions of emergence might trigger an attitude of inadequacy and hesitancy.

To strengthen the first impulse and inhibit the second we have endeavored to put the argument forward as concretely as possible, almost as if to create the illusion that it could be put into practice tomorrow morning. But this certainly does not preclude an awareness of the battle that would need to be waged. It is one thing to bring together the building blocks of the issue and quite another to join with other actors in designing an effective way forward.[19]

Yet the theme has already taken an important step. It has broken conspiracies of silence, gathered forces, indicated further changes.

Our goal in these pages is to provide this nascent shift in opinion—and its multiple ramifications in the political and union system, the mass media, in the governance and government of the country, and even in international public opinion—with a reasoned guide complete with recipes.

At the end of the day, other countries within the European Union have at some point in their history raised key issues of national interest—think of German reunification or successive rounds of community enlargement. So why should Italy not do so, when the issue also affects other countries and plays an important role in building the community?

---

[19] From within the set of problems just laid out, it is possible to construct a daily exercise to understand which way the wind is blowing. It consists of asking oneself about the probable effects of this or that economic development or measure on the degree of economic submergence. Since we are dealing with a precarious balance between the two markets--regular and irregular--repeatedly posing this question and confronting it with the reality of the facts develops a concrete perception with respect to the evolution of the phenomenon that resembles the stylus of the seismograph.

9. First Report of the National Committee for the Emergence of Unregulated Labor by the Presidency of the Council of Ministers[*]

In preparation for the decrees in connection with the 2000 Finance Bill, the following interim fact sheets are aimed at initiating a consideration of possible measures in favor of emergence. They concern only certain forms of undeclared work and economic activity—those for which it is possible, at this time to express a reasoned opinion. They have been developed from within the current frame of reference (of European and national legislation, government policy, and economic and social trends), but they also aim to smooth out corners and pave the way for a broader rearrangement.

It is worthwhile by way of introduction, to establish some points of reference:

- The emergence of partly or completely undeclared businesses and labor is a multifaceted issue that needs to be addressed comprehensively.
- Often, the relevant measures affect vast sectors of workers—they are designed in such a way as to alleviate their condition of illegality.
- And yet the planned financial outlays are small—sometimes they are small investments meant to reinforce

* From: Meldolesi, L. (2022), *Protagonismi mediterranei,* pp. 65-80. Originally published as Comitato Nazionale per l'emersione del lavoro non regolare [National Committee for the Emergence of Unregulated Labor] (1999), *Prima relazione,* November 30. Earlier versions of this report were discussed at the National Committee and at several meetings with representatives of the social partners and civil society and with working groups at the Milan Chamber of Commerce, the Universities of Naples and Bari, and Aiccre in Palermo. The resulting picture is interlocutory in nature but can be taken as a starting point for certain legislative initiatives.

the current trend toward emergence, from which the public treasury and social security stand to benefit.

- The goal is to open a perspective, as far as possible coherent, on which to bring together the myriad initiatives currently arising around the topic — this is a goal that must be pursued vigorously.
- This is a policy under construction that will require broad social and institutional participation and must keep pace with the other aspects of the project.

Possible Initial Measures for Emergence

1. Dr. Rossi of the Ministry of Finance, a member of the Committee, has suggested a legislative provision that would allow very small businesses to pay their tax liabilities at a flat rate rather than in proportion to their volume of business. Currently this is allowed up to a maximum of 20 million of turnover. This threshold should be raised and should perhaps allow a complete exemption from VAT.

This proposal is supported by the existence of similar legislation in some European partner countries (and by the opinion of influential international institutions). In France, for example, entrepreneurs who do not exceed a turnover of 50 million annually are exempt from various tax and social security obligations. The measure, as Dr. Rossi pointed out, would affect 1.5 million "small and very small businesses" The state would benefit because it would recover small amounts that are difficult to collect, it would get on top of related litigation, it would be able to use the designated personnel elsewhere, and entrepreneurs would at once be freed from tax worries and from much of the corresponding compliance costs.

(There are, however, some drawbacks. If the existing fiscal regime, for example were extended *sic et simpliciter* up to 20 million of turnover — which entails calculating profit and payable

VAT on a flat-rate basis and applying a different percentage to the production of goods and services—more firms would have no interest in requesting invoices from their suppliers, because they would not be deducting them from either VAT or revenues—they would prefer to obtain lower prices. In addition, more enterprises would have no interest in invoicing the goods and services produced so as not to exceed the predetermined limit. Finally, while the condition of very small entrepreneurs would improve—which would undoubtedly favor the process of emergence—it would not necessarily induce a process of regularization of employee labor because the flat rate of taxation does not include labor-related benefits. In conclusion, a lump-sum taxation that favors emergence should be studied—for example, lowering the percentage in the case of hiring. A clear framework should be drawn that provides for standard consequences, without hypocrisy, and finally, a monitoring and evaluation system, such as the one envisaged in sub 4, should be created that can keep the described reality "at bay").

2. It is possible to study other *tax and contribution mechanisms* of a general, sectoral or territorial nature favorable to business and labor regularization.

For example, newly registered businesses, Dr. Rossi suggests, could enjoy a tax exemption for two years and be supervised by a tax tutor who would help them keep accounting records and adapt to with current administrative procedures. In addition, with modest investment, as Dr. Brunello of the Ministry of Finance points out, it would be possible to modify the sectorial fiscal studies to focus them on emergence, through differentiated tax deductions for those who hire. In this regard, it is necessary to be able to figure out, by sector and turnover, what the "low barrier" to overcome is, starting from the level

171

just above sub 1. (According to a calculation based on the artisans of the Spanish Quarters in Naples, the undeclared income of an employee actually "covers" the partial undeclared income of the employer, so that if one wanted to regularize a single worker helping an artisan for five years the cost, truly prohibitive, would be 80 million lire).

Recent successes in combating income and social security tax evasion (and more generally the degree to which the country's economy is submerged) have allowed an important step forward. If the courage existed to reinvest a small percentage of those proceeds into a regularization effort (building or strengthening, in parallel, tax mechanisms and contributory emergence), it would be possible to continue and vigorously expand the virtuous circle that has been started. The underlying idea is that of a friendly state that "doesn't get played" — that is, a state that dispenses trust, cooperation, escape routes, etc., but only until there is proof to the contrary, and which, in order to head this off, continuously updates a database of each citizen's benefits and fiscal behavior.

3. Favorable treatment could be established for "old-age" pensioners (within a certain income and pension limit).

Rationale
- The pensions actually received are often insufficient to support an acceptable standard of living, while running a small business can be a health benefit.
- A consequence of the widespread use of the new contributory system is that those who get a pension have already (mostly) contributed to building it — their subsequent work does not play a major role in it. Thus, following prevailing legislation in Europe, the ban for all old-age pensions on the combination of

pension and work would have to be abolished (and the current 50 percent reduction in the contributions of retired artisans could be replaced by a simple exemption with the consequent abolition of related bureaucratic costs, both public and private).

– It is not reasonable to attribute (implicitly) the same presumption of taxable income to a craftsman in his prime and an elderly craftsman – this results in the latter being severely penalized.

– The contribution of elderly retirees is nevertheless national income that should not be underestimated (It is erroneous to think that it might actually "displace" young people's labor).

– On the contrary, society gains an additional benefit because old people's work spontaneously promotes the transfer of knowledge to younger people (and could be reconciled with the gradual work reduction and hand-off schemes between old and young that are under discussion).

– Once reevaluated, better use could be made of the labor of senior craftsmen (or rather some of them) in experimental institutions that combine new knowledge with old (codified knowledge with tacit knowledge).

– A measure of this nature could enjoy a wide consensus in an area with rapid proportional population growth.

4. As noted, the measures discussed so far (and many of those that follow) can be feedback loops. For example, who can assure us that the actual turnover is as stated and not five to ten times higher? The tax relief obviously makes sense if the *control system* is able to prevent such eventualities. If this is deemed unlikely as things stand, an ad hoc system with spot checks exceeding a certain percentage threshold of the total (and with

fines at a progressive rate relative to the amount of evasion) will need to be put in place. In addition, it is important to keep the described reality under continuous observation (monitoring) and carry out evaluations of the measures at regular intervals that allow for their improvement as we go along.

5. *Realignment contracts* are considered a main instrument of emergence policies. There are in this regard recent fact-finding investigations by the Ministry of Labor and the Carabinieri task force that add to well-known trade union and university-based publications. (The experience of the province of Lecce has also been proposed to the Brussels Commission as a 'best practice' regarding the Plan for Employment). Created as an agreement between the social partners, realignment contracts have developed through a series of provisions that have been extended up to now.

The problem is how to strengthen this policy intervention, expand it and finally turn it into a real policy of emergence based on a specially tailored body of legislation. As a starting point, the following points may be noted.

a) There is a willingness on the part of the minister to apply benefits that will encourage entrepreneurs to carry through with them, instead of just continuing along at a halfway point. (The fact that this has not yet been put into practice is probably due to the need not to jeopardize the Brussels package about which we shall say more below).

b) It is often forgotten that existing realignment contracts are concentrated by sector and especially territorially. In non-agricultural activities, they cover those areas (unfortunately a minority in the South) where the collective culture suggests that, at least formally, workers should come into compliance. In order to build a pension for themselves, workers will accept even severe wage cuts. That is why there is a problem of wage realignment, not pension realignment. (Indeed, from the point of view of the INPS [National Institute of Social Security], these are workers in good standing for all intents and purposes, to the extent that they should therefore be counted as regular).

But what can be done about the vast majority of the undeclared (the *fully submerged*) who have so far not considered these contracts? Instead of approaching them from the wage side, recalls Dr. Massicci of the Treasury and member of the Committee, they could be approached from the *pension* angle.

In this regard, Part 23 of Law 196/1997 already provides that for three years "notional contributions may be credited, for the purpose of the eligibility and amount of the pension." Since INPS is substantially increasing its revenues (presumably from the informal economy), it would be possible on an experimental basis to use a small portion of it to begin applying this provision. This would be a lure that would entice workers in a given experimental area to emerge—it would push them to regularize and begin paying contributions. For example, a notional pro-emergence contribution for 3-5 years could push the age group "starting a family" (20-30-year-olds, whom the measure would primarily target) to strive for a regular retirement.

(c) This important step could be combined with the wage initiative as well as others. In reviewing the experience, some protagonists of realignment contracts complain about the absence of the local public authority from such initiatives. The issue, they argue, cannot be resolved between the social partners alone—within a legislative framework favorable to emergence, it should be possible to address local development problems.

This would involve launching *territorial pacts aimed at emergence* (linked, perhaps, to existing pacts), providing for the establishment on the ground of special *development centers* (aimed at capacity building, institution building), based on a small number of skilled technicians with fixed-term contracts, linked to cultural and policy institutes. Backed by the established regional and provincial Commissions for Emergence, these centers should:

- support the process of emergence by involving for this purpose local governments and the offices of the national administrations present in the area;
- find specific solutions appropriate to concrete situations (e.g. regarding arbitration between the parties, litigation with the state, relocation, etc.);
- play a mentoring role in the process of emergence of businesses, stimulating sectoral and inter-sectoral associations, facilitating technological change, improving access to markets, etc.;
- rationalize and increase the effectiveness-efficiency of area intervention policies;
- build real public planning in the area.
- With modest funding, these kinds of territorial pacts, together with their (centrally linked) development centers, could significantly elevate the overall performance of local public spending, both directly and indirectly, because of the abundant economic-social energy they could gradually mobilize.

6. Italy has recently obtained a commitment from the European Commission for a "preamble" *statement* regarding the Decision on Employment Guidelines for 2000 in which the "function of the guidelines with reference to the problem of illegal work, as an area for intervention" will be recognized.

There is, on the other hand, an understandable expectation in our country about whether the *three-year exemption* provided by the EU for new employment will be extended to the undeclared who regularize. This measure has so far been denied, although the government has resumed negotiations. There is also, in this regard, a very simple alternative to the extension of benefits (suggested by Dr. Ceriani of the Ministry of Finance) — which is to consider the emergence of labor *sic et simpliciter* as new employment from an administrative point of view.

More generally, the vexed question of "state aid" could be interpreted in a different way. Up to now, the EU has allowed tax and contribution differentials between countries, but not within each country. Yet indirect economic policy of this kind can be of great significance, as shown for example, by the US experience. Could we not find a narrow lane, an alleyway perhaps, that snakes between these two "facts"? Of course we cannot go back to taxing social security contributions. We need to come up with more useful and effective ways — precisely in the vein of extending benefits for new employment, designating what is regularized as new, de-taxing profits, temporarily exempting certain areas of intensive intervention, etc.

7. In agriculture there has been a major growth in realignment contracts (which for this sector are extended to the entire country). The related issue is the one discussed above, with additional specifics that will need to be explored further with the institutions and social partners involved.

In addition, in this industry the famous 51 days worked annually has in the past been a popular expedient for accessing the minimum threshold of social security contributions. Abuse has since been reduced, although not eradicated. With this social security coverage, the worker can allocate his or her activity elsewhere, appearing as an agricultural employee but actually working off the books on a daily basis. Area crossings between property, land, production and labor can be experimented with to improve the situation. Combined with allowances sub 1 and 3 they could bring some of the reality in question into the open.

Finally, there is widespread irregularity in occasional agricultural work (done mostly by non-EU nationals). Sometimes, explains Dr. Serino of the Ministry of Agriculture and a member of the Committee, it is simple circumvention. For example, a farmer has five days to temporarily enroll an employee. But often the harvest is completed in five days. One approach to this could be temporary regularization services provided by municipalities. (Again, a simplified flat-rate system could be used here, perhaps with an exemption for very small farmers.)

8. It should be added at this point that the process of emergence from irregular labor can also develop into a process of regularization of *non-EU* labor. It could be established that the "emerging" non-EU worker would be entered automatically (along with the employer) on a standby list available to the authorities and that his or her position would be gradually regularized *ad personam* (by a single ad hoc center, to which all related information and the necessary monitoring at regular intervals would be reported) in two to three years of tax payments.

9. Specific emergence problems also exist in other sectors, such as personal services, commerce, construction and tourism — sectors with a very high incidence of undeclared labor (with a tendency to worsen moving south). Undeclared domestic labor is a vast archipelago (on the order of many hundreds of thousands of people). On an experimental basis, as part of the legislative efforts in this regard being undertaken by Parliament, certain

tax deductions — reserved for families with handicapped, chronically ill or young children — could be linked to the regularization of their caregivers. The effect would be positive if there were a balance between the deduction and the flat rate. For example, an "au pair" could be entitled to one million a month plus two hundred thousand lire in contributions (to be paid two or three times a year through postal slips). If the family could deduct what they paid from their taxable income, the operation would be worthwhile. Once successful, this "wedge" of regularity could be extended with other solicitations, such as through unions collecting instances of regularization of employees, focusing monitoring on the middle- and upper-income brackets, etc.

For *trade*, where there is a vast underground, progressive regularization could be linked to the current liberalization process, getting the trade associations involved. The difficulty lies in the fact that owners often tend toward under-invoicing in order to conceal part of their income and therefore, quite apart from contribution expenses, they have no interest in regularizing those employees who would suggest that the owner's income is higher than what is declared. Note here the importance of working *a coté* with the Ministry of Finance (as with sub 1 and 2). In fact, considering the way sectorial fiscal studies are structured, comparing business trends in different areas and the fine tuning of controls can be as decisive for the tax authorities as for the emergence of undeclared work.

In addition, in public *construction* there is an initial safeguard in the Merloni law against overbidding in contracts. It might be added that part of the inspections should be directed specifically toward such eventualities. In contrast, private construction (like commerce and other sectors) requires spot checks (such as those mentioned under 4) that reach a threshold that makes the administrative authorities' action credible.

Alternatively, it could be controlled per square meter of construction or renovation.

Finally, in *tourism*, the unemployment benefit given to employees because of the seasonal nature of their work unfortunately lends itself to abuse. It is often convenient for both employer and employee to undertake notional seasonal layoffs in order to access the benefits. Probably, an alternative should be sought in a disaggregated study of the relationship between hotel attendance and employment, in support for the lengthening of the tourist season, and in related advantages—not least for workers, who may be encouraged through tax and contribution channels to extend their regular employment.

10. Much undeclared work has behind it an acquired social security position (private or public) or a state benefit. Sometimes, out of calculation or fear, it is the wage earner who prefers irregularity—to get higher wages or not to lose an advantage (real or presumed). In all these cases it is illusory to seek the Ariadne's thread of legalization without addressing the problem.

One way to do this may be to *"capitalize" the subsidy* (of unemployment, layoff, socially useful labor, retirement pension, etc.), that is, to turn it into a grant to help the worker start his or her own business activity. Taking advantage of the present rather low interest rates, this capitalization, backed by appropriate banking agreements, can significantly increase the capital initially available to the worker. In addition, such measures can be combined with enterprise creation (e.g., honor loans).

Another way to go is to embrace the current process of *revising* social safety nets to reduce and perhaps neutralize, measure by measure, their "submerging consequences" A third is to eliminate some institutions. For example, job placement offices have no real role in market functioning (indeed, in this regard, it can be easily and efficiently replaced) but it certifies small advantages that produce the unwanted effect of inducing people to go underground. (The provision of other, "submersion-free" benefits should be studied as an alternative.) A fourth way is to repeal some prohibitions, such as the one that prevents public employees from working a second job. Alternative trajectories could be created, such as better-paid full-time work and public half-time that can combine with regular private half-time.

However, it is always wrong (indeed hypocritical) to think that a working-age person with a low income who has a salary, allowance or pension and who has time available, is not attracted to underground work.

11. A great deal of existing legislation was put in place without taking into account the existence of the dual labor market (regular and irregular). But actually, the boundary separating the two markets is very sensitive and fluid — so that concerning any provision, we can predict whether and how much it will produce a submerging or emergent effect. This means that a coherent policy of emergence inevitably requires a gradual rearrangement of existing regulations.

Sometimes it is not at all easy to point the way. Under the law, most salaried employees can take on extra work of an occasional nature. But it does not benefit either the employer or the worker to report this type of employment relationship. The former would have to pay social security contributions, while the latter would have to pay taxes. And in fact, there are many actual cases of this double detriment to the state. How to react? One way is to move to a higher level of public and social scrutiny. Another would be, under different sectoral and territorial conditions, to experimentally exempt one of the parties from the obligation of the law so as to ascertain whether this would undermine the current convergence of interests. A third way, perhaps the most reasonable, is to act on both these fronts.

12. The efficiency and effectiveness of the state are of great importance to our topic. Some of the present difficulties are the effect of past laxity, while the current improvement in the tax and contribution situation is undoubtedly an effect of the efforts made in this regard. Another decisive factor has been the calming of the social climate, which is now more favorable to regulation and regular behavior as compared with the past. Nevertheless, there is still a long way to go in improving the performance of administrations, making them more aware of what is at stake, linking them to the needs of citizens and, at the same time, orienting society toward a more regular way of living and working.

A useful stratagem could be the introduction of *certification* for access to public subsidies at all levels, obtainable upon request by businesses that demonstrate compliance with labor safety, child labor and adult labor legislation. Such certification could also be granted to enterprises that begin the process of wage or pension realignment but would be automatically suspended if it were discontinued.

It is true, on the other hand, as the "Third Italy" experience has shown, that economic expansion and increased productivity are often decisive levers for emergence. Within current economic-political constraints and development policies (such as those of the National Labor Plan, Agenda 2000, Dps, Sviluppo Italia, etc.) it is necessary to strengthen especially *the local level of intervention*. As mentioned, the consolidation and growth of sectoral-territorial competitive advantages, the development of associationism, cooperation, productive and commercial consortia, credit consortia, technological change, and economies external to enterprises (but internal to the site) are part and parcel of the problem. Based on a careful assessment of what has been done and what is envisioned, these key features could receive further legislative encouragement. Finally, there is the issue of area intervention for development and emergence, which has already received some interest (Meldolesi, Ruvolo, Caianiello, Voltura, Becattini, Marino, Baculo) and which may soon find application, at least experimentally.

BIBLIOGRAPHY

Adizes, I. (1988) *Corporate Lifecycles*, Englewood NJ, Prentice

Aquino, A. (1996) *I termini essenziali del problema Mezzogiorno*, paper presented at the Annual Conference of the Società Italiana degli Economisti, Bologna.

Artus, I. (1998) *Industrial Relations in Eastern Germany Aiming at Equalization – Achieving Differentiation*, mimeo

Bàculo, L. (1997) "Segni di industrializzazione leggera nel Mezzogiorno", in *Stato e mercato*, n. 3.

Bàculo, L., ed. (1994) *Impresa forte, politica debole. Imprenditori di successo nel Mezzogiorno*, Napoli, ISI.

Banfield, E. (1958) *The Moral Bases of a Backward Society*, New York, Free Press.

Bassetti, P. (2015) *Svegliamoci Italici!* Vnezia, Marsilio

Becattini, G. (1996) "I sistemi locali nello sviluppo economico italiano e nella sua interpretazione." *Sviluppo locale*, II-III, n. 2-3.

Bianchi, T. (1999) "Intervento Straordinario REvisited. A Research Proposal", mimeo.

Bluhm, K. (1998) *The Reconstruction of Inter-Firms and Extra-Firms Cooperation in the East-German Transition: Obstructive or Innovative?* Mimeo.

Bodo, G. and Viesti, G. (1997) *La grande svolta*, Roma, Donzelli

Braudel, F. (1980) *Civilization matérielle, Economie et Capitalisme (XV-XVII siècle)* Paris, Colin

Braudel, F. (1981) *La dinamica del capitalismo*, Bologna, Il Mulino

Bufalino, G. and Zago, N. (1993) *Cento Sicilie*, Firenze, La Nuova Italia.

Carzaniga, A. (2021) "Testo preliminare per una nuova politica per il Mezzogiorno", *Italia Vulcanica 11: La montagna e il topolino*, Roma, IDE.

Cassano, F. (1996) *Il pensiero meridiano*, Roma-Bari, Laterza.

Centorrino, M. and Signorino, G. (1997) *Macroeconomia della mafia*, Firenze, La Nuova Italia.

Colorni, E. (1975) "Dell'antropomorfismo nelle scienze" in *Scritti*, ed. by N. Bobbio, Firenze, La Nuova Italia. English translation, "On Anthropomorphism in the Sciences", in Colorni, E. and Spinelli, A. (2020) *Dialogues*, New York, Bordighera Press.

Colorni, E. and Spinelli, A. (2020) *Dialogues*, New York, Bordighera Press.

Comitato Nazionale per l'emersione del lavoro non regolare (1999) *Prima relazione*, November 30.

D'Antonio M. (1991) "Il nemico è l'assistenzialismo", *Mondo Economico*, 20 luglio.

De Cecco, M. (1999) *Berlin Diary*, mimeo.

Di Nola, P. (2000) *Difficile ma possibile. Una valutazione della L. 44/86 per l'imprenditorialità giovanile*, Napoli, ESI.

Dickie, J. (1999) "Stereotipi del Sud d'Italia, 1860-1900" in Lumley, R. and Morris, J., eds., *Oltre il meridionalismo*, Roma, Carocci.

Festinger L. (1957) *A Therory of Cognitive Dissonance*, Stanford, Ca, Stanford UP.

Galli G. and Onado M. (1990) "Dualismo territoriale e sistema finanziario", in Banca d'Italia, *Il sistema finanziario del Mezzogiorno*, Roma, Banca d'Italia.

Gaudino, S. (1998) "Costumi da bagno a Gragnano. Origini e sviluppo di una vocazione produttiva locale", in Meldolesi, L. and Aniello, V. (eds.) *L'Italia che non c'è: quant'è, dov'è, com'è?* special issue of *Rivista di politica economica*, n. viii-ix.

German Brief (1998) *Manufacturing Revival*, vol. X, n. 20.

Gerschenkron, A. (1961) *Economic Backwardness in Historical Perspective*, Cambridge MA, Harvard UP.

Gladwell, M. (1999) *The Tipping Point. How Little Things Can Make a Big Difference*, Boston, Little.

Goethe, J. W. (2014) *Massime e riflessioni*, Milano, Il Sole 24 Ore.

Gore, A. (1993) *Reinventing Government*, Washington D.C.

Gribaudi, G. (1999) "Le immagini del Mezzogiorno", in Lumley, R. and Morris, J., eds., *Oltre il meridionalismo*, Roma, Carocci.

Hirschman, A.O. (1958) *The Strategy of Economic Development*, New Haven, Conn., Yale UP.

Hirschman A.O. (1965) "Obstacles to Development: A Classification and a Quasi-Vanishing Act", *Economic Development and Cultural Change*, July; now in Hirschman (1971).

Hirschman A.O. (1971) *A Bias for Hope*, New Haven, Conn., Yale UP.

Hirschman A.O. (1973) "The Changing Tolerance for Income Inequality in the Course of Economic Development", *Quarterly Journal of Economics*, December.

Hirschman, A. O. (1981) *Essays in Trespassing. Economics to Politics and Beyond*, Cambridge UK, Cambridge UP.

Hirschman A.O. (1982) *Shifting Involvements: Private Interest and Public Action*, Princeton NJ, Princeton UP.

Hirschman, A.O. (1986) *Rival Views of Market Society and Other Recent Essays*, New York, Viking.

Hirschman, A.O. (1990) "The Case Against One Thing at a Time", in *World Development*, December.

Hirschman, A.O. (1995) *A Propensity for Self-subversion*, Cambridge MA, Harvard UP.

Hulten, C.R. (1994) *Optional Growth and Infrastructure. Capital Theory and Implications for Empirical Modelling*. Mimeo.

Hirschman, A.O. and Lindblom, C.E. (1962) "Economic Development, Research and Development, Policy Making: Some Converging Views", in *Behavioral Science*, April.

Iannuzzo, A. (1990) *Teoria e pratica dei progetti di sviluppo. Il caso del disinquinamento del golfo di Napoli*, degree dissertation, University of Naples.

Incisa di Camerana, L. (1996) *L'Italia ha vinto la terza guerra mondiale*, Bari, Laterza.

IPR Marketing (1996) "Sondaggio realizzato per l'Osservatorio Permanente sull'Opinione pubblica di Napoli".

Italia Vulcanica 1 (2018) *Qui comincia l'avventura*. Roma: IDE.

Italia Vulcanica 2 (2019) *L'alta marea, cronache dall'Italia vulcanica*. Roma: IDE.

Italia Vulcanica 3 (2019) *Il Mezzogiorno della speranza*. Roma, IDE.

Italia Vulcanica 4 (2020) *Mal di crescita*. Roma: IDE.

Italia Vulcanica 5 (2020) *Bingo!* Roma: IDE.

Italia Vulcanica 6-7 (2020) *Montagne russe*. Roma: IDE.

Italia Vulcanica 8 (2020) *Avant le deluge*. Roma: IDE.

Italia Vulcanica 9 (2020) *Napoli oh cara*. Roma: IDE.

Italia Vulcanica 10 (2021) *Dall'alto della Cabina*. Roma: IDE.

Italia Vulcanica 11 (2021c) *La montagna e il topolino*. Roma: IDE.

Italia Vulcanica 12-13 (2022) *Il coraggio dell'innocenza*. Roma: IDE.

Locke, R. and Trigilia, C. (1998) *Mirror Images? Political Strategies for Economic Development in Eastern Germany and Southern Italy*, mimeo.

Macry, P. (1999) "L'occasione meridionale", in *Il Mulino*, n. 5.

189

Mc Kinnon, R.L. (1963) "Optimum Currency Areas", in *The American Economic Review*, September.

Meldolesi, L. (1984) "'Economia critica' e 'Storia della lunga durata'. Un'introduzione", in *Inchiesta*, n. 64-5.

Meldolesi, L. (1985) "America, America: note su Hirschman, Hartz e Brudel", in *Inchiesta*, n. 69.

Meldolesi, L. (1990) "Mezzogiorno con gioia", in Nord e Sud, n. 2. Reprinted in Meldolesi, L. (2021) *Mezzogiorno con gioia!* Soveria Mannelli, Rubbettino.

Meldolesi, L. (1992a) *Spender meglio è possibile*, Bologna, Il Mulino.

Meldolesi, L. (1992b) "Dietro le quinte di una Strategia", *Studi economici*, n. 2.

Meldolesi, L. (1993a) "Sicilia aiutati", in *Cooperazione*, n. 9.

Meldolesi, L. (1993b) "Valutazione e buon governo. Un primo bilancio". Mimeo.

Meldolesi, L. (1994a) "Come sospingere il Mezzogiorno verso l'Europa", in *Il Mulino*, n. 2.

Meldolesi, L. (1994b) Alla *scoperta del possibile. Il mondo sorprendente di Albert O. Hirschman*, Bologna, Il Mulino. English translation: *Discovering the Possible. The surprising world of Albert O. Hirschman*, Notre Dame IN, Notre Dame UP, 1955.

Meldolesi, L. (1994c) "Sulla nozione di squilibrio ottimo", in Caravale, G., ed., *Equilibrio e teoria economica*, Bologna, Il Mulino.

Meldolesi, L. (1994d) "Democrazia e intransigenza: un lamento post-elettorale", *Il Mulino*, XLIII, n. 3.

Meldolesi, L. (1995) *Discovering the Possible: The Surprising World of Albert Hirschman*, Notre Dame, IN, Notre Dame UP.

Meldolesi, L. (1996a) "L'elevata mobilità del lavoro nel Mezzogiorno della speranza", in Galli, G, ed., *La mobilità della società italiana. Le persone, le imprese, le istituzioni*, Roma, Sipi. Reprinted in Meldolesi, L. (2021c) *Mezzogiorno con gioia!* Soveria Mannelli, Rubbettino.

Meldolesi, L. (1996 b) "I cento gamberi", in *Economia e politica industriale*, n. 90.

Meldolesi, L. (1996c) "Uno schema per il Sud", in *Economia e politica industriale*, n.90; reprinted in Meldolesi, L. (2021c) *Mezzogiorno con gioia!* Soveria Mannelli, Rubbettino.

Meldolesi, L. (1998a) *Dalla parte del Sud*, Bari-Roma, Laterza.

Meldolesi, L. (1998b) "Schema base per un progetto di emersione", in Del Prete, E. Mariti, P. and Vellere, M.A. (eds.) (1998) "L'economia italiana tra centralità europea e marginalità mediterranea", *Quaderni del Dipartimento per lo studio delle società mediterranee dell'Università degli Studi di Bari*, no. 17, Bari.

Meldolesi, L. (2000) *Occupazione e emersione*, Roma, Carocci.

Meldolesi, L. (2001) *Sud, liberare lo sviluppo*, Roma, Carocci.

Meldolesi, L. (2010) *Milano-Napoli. Prove di dialogo federalista*, Napoli, Guida.

Meldolesi, L. (2020a) *Eppur si può!* Soveria Mannelli, Rubbettino.

Meldolesi, L. (2020b) "Prime idee per lo sviluppo locale del Mezzogiorno". In *Montagne russe, Italia Vulcanica* n. 6-7.

Meldolesi, L. (2021a) *Mezzogiorno. Mezzomondo*, Soveria Mannelli, Rubbettino.

Meldolesi, L. (2021b) "Presentazione", *Italia Vulcanica 11: La montagna e il topolino*, Roma, IDE.

Meldolesi, L. (2021c) *Mezzogiorno con gioia!* Soveria Mannelli, Rubbettino.

Meldolesi, L. (2022) *Protagonismi mediterranei*, Soveria Mannelli, Rubbettino.

Meldolesi, L. and Stame, N. (1995) "Intervento diretto dello Stato e coinvolgimento dei beneficiari: alcune lezioni economiche della legge sull'imprenditorialità giovanile", in *L'industria*, vol. xiv, n. 4.

Meldolesi, L., Arbitrio, A. and Del Monaco, M.B. (1996) "Lavoro e uscita-voce nel quarilatero di Grumo Nevano", in *Economia Marche*, n. 3. Reprinted in Meldolesi, L. (2021) *Mezzogiorno. Mezzomondo*, Soveria Mannelli, Rubbettino.

Meldolesi, L. and Aniello, V., ed. (1998) "Un'Italia che non c'è: quant'è, dov'è, com'è", in *Rivista di Politica Economica*, August-September, October-November.

Moe, N. (1999) "Il Sud di Giovanni Verga tra la Sicilia Pittoresca e la questione meridionale", in Lumley, R. and Morris, J., eds., *Oltre il meridionalismo*, Roma, Carocci.

Mundell, R. (1961) "A Theory of Optimum Currency Area ", in *The American Economic Review*, September.

Nicolaus, O. (1996) "A proposito del pensiero meridiano", in *Pluriverso*, n. 3.

Osborne, D. and Gaebler, T. (1992) *Reinventing Government. How the Entrepreneurial Spirit is Transforming the Public Sector*, New York, Penguin.

Padoa-Schioppa F. (1988a) "Strategie e tecniche d'intervento", in Progetto finalizzato CNR, *Struttura ed evoluzione dell'economia italiana*, Roma, CNR.

Padoa-Schioppa F. (1988b) "Intervento" al Convegno *Il Mezzogiorno e il '92*, Gruppo Democratico e Liberale al Parlamento Europeo, Napoli 19 dicembre 1988a.

Peyrefitte, A. (1998) *Du 'miracle' en économie*, Paris, Jacob.

Pezzino, P. (1992) *Il paradiso abitato dai diavoli*, Milano, Franco Angeli.

Putnam, R.D. (1993) *Making Democracy Work*, Priceton NJ, Princeton UP.

Rossi Doria, M. (1982) *Scritti sul Mezzogiorno*, Torino, Einaudi.

Salamon, S. L., ed. (1989) *Beyond Privatization. The Tools of Government Action*, Washington D.C., The Urban Institute Press.

Sales, I. (1999) *Il Sud al tempo dell'euro*, Roma, Editori Riuniti.

Sarcinelli, M. (1989) "Mezzogiorno e mercato unico europeo: complementarità e o conflitti di obiettivi", *Moneta e credito* vol. 42, n. 166.

Scitovsky, T. (1958) *Economic Theory and Western Economic Integration*, London, Unwin.

Scitovsky, T. (1976) *The Joyless Economy. An Inquiry into Human Satisfaction and Consumer Dissatisfaction*, Oxford, Oxford UP.

Serao, M. (1994) *Il ventre di Napoli*, Napoli, Casa Editrice Luca Torre.

Silone, I. (1968) *Emergency Exit*, New York, Harper.

Stame, N., ed. (2024) *An Education*, New York, Bordighera Press

Tagle, L. (1992) *La politica comunitaria in Campania*, degree dissertation, University of Naples.

Trigilia, C. (1992) *Sviluppo senza autonomia*, Bologna, Il Mulino.

Viesti, G. (1996) "Europa, Italia, Mezzogiorno. Caratteristiche e possibili effetti del processo di integrazione", in *Economia italiana*, n. 2.

INDEX OF NAMES

About the Editor

NICOLETTA STAME, sociologist: MA at SUNY — Binghamton; Assistant Professor at Paris X, Messina, Bari; Professor at Sapienza University of Roma until 2010.

Presently, she is Vice President of A Colorni-Hirschman International Institute. She is interested in democratic policies of development, particularly in the Mezzogiorno, also from the perspective of their evaluation that she approaches through a "possibilist" lens. She is past President of Associazione Italiana di Valutazione and of European Evaluation Society, and board member of *Evaluation*. Her published books in English are: *From Studies to Streams* (with R. Rist), *The Evaluation Enterprise* (with J.-E. Furubo), *Ethics for Evaluation: beyond "Doing no Harm" to "Tackling Bad and "Doing Good"* (with R. van den Berg and P. Hawkins), *Possibilism and Evaluation: Albert Hirschman and Judith Tendler*.

IL NOSTRO MEZZOGIORNO

This series is dedicated to new perspectives on how we might [re-]consider Southern Italy and the Mediterranean.

Luca Meldolesi. *An America in Antiquity? Mediterranean Perspectives: "La pensée de midi" and "Our Mezzogiorno"*. ISBN 978-1-59954-207-2

Nicoletta Stame, ed. *An Education: Selected Writings by Luca Meldolesi and Friends*. ISBN 978-1-59954-226-3

www.ingramcontent.com/pod-product-compliance
Lightning Source LLC
Chambersburg PA
CBHW031431270326
41930CB00007B/653